Poems and New Poems

by

Francis Thompson

The Echo Library 2007

Published by

The Echo Library

Echo Library
131 High St.
Teddington
Middlesex TW11 8HH

www.echo-library.com

Please report serious faults in the text to complaints@echo-library.com

ISBN 978-1-4068-2312-7

POEMS

CONTENTS

Dedication	1
Love in Dian's Lap	
Before Her Portrait in Youth	2
To a Poet Breaking Silence	4
Manus Animam Pinxit	6
A Carrier-Song	8
Scala Jacobi Portaque Eburnea	11
Gilded Gold	12
Her Portrait	14
Epilogue—To The Poet's Sitter,	18
Miscellaneous Poems	
To the Dead Cardinal of Westminster	20
A Fallen Yew	25
Dream-Tryst	28
A Corymbus for Autumn	29
The Hound of Heaven	33
A Judgment in Heaven	38
Poems on Children	
Daisy	43
The Making of Viola	45
To My Godchild	48
To Poppy	50
To Monica Thought Dying	53

DEDICATION—TO WILFRID AND ALICE MEYNELL

If the rose in meek duty
May dedicate humbly
To her grower the beauty
Wherewith she is comely;
If the mine to the miner
The jewels that pined in it,
Earth to diviner
The springs he divined in it;
To the grapes the wine-pitcher
Their juice that was crushed in it,
Viol to its witcher
The music lay hushed in it;
If the lips may pay Gladness
In laughters she wakened,
And the heart to its sadness
Weeping unslakened,
If the hid and sealed coffer,
Whose having not his is,
To the loosers may proffer
Their finding—here this is;
Their lives if all livers
To the Life of all living, -
To you, O dear givers!
I give your own giving.

BEFORE HER PORTRAIT IN YOUTH

As lovers, banished from their lady's face
And hopeless of her grace,
Fashion a ghostly sweetness in its place,
Fondly adore
Some stealth-won cast attire she wore,
A kerchief or a glove:
And at the lover's beck
Into the glove there fleets the hand,
Or at impetuous command
Up from the kerchief floats the virgin neck:
So I, in very lowlihead of love, -
Too shyly reverencing
To let one thought's light footfall smooth
Tread near the living, consecrated thing, -
Treasure me thy cast youth.
This outworn vesture, tenantless of thee,
Hath yet my knee,
For that, with show and semblance fair
Of the past Her
Who once the beautiful, discarded raiment bare,
It cheateth me.
As gale to gale drifts breath
Of blossoms' death,
So dropping down the years from hour to hour
This dead youth's scent is wafted me to-day:
I sit, and from the fragrance dream the flower.
So, then, she looked (I say);
And so her front sunk down
Heavy beneath the poet's iron crown:
On her mouth museful sweet -
(Even as the twin lips meet)
Did thought and sadness greet:
Sighs
In those mournful eyes
So put on visibilities;
As viewless ether turns, in deep on deep, to dyes.
Thus, long ago,
She kept her meditative paces slow
Through maiden meads, with waved shadow and gleam
Of locks half-lifted on the winds of dream,
Till love up-caught her to his chariot's glow.
Yet, voluntary, happier Proserpine!
This drooping flower of youth thou lettest fall

I, faring in the cockshut-light, astray,
Find on my 'lated way,
And stoop, and gather for memorial,
And lay it on my bosom, and make it mine.
To this, the all of love the stars allow me,
I dedicate and vow me.
I reach back through the days
A trothed hand to the dead the last trump shall not raise.
The water-wraith that cries
From those eternal sorrows of thy pictured eyes
Entwines and draws me down their soundless intricacies!

TO A POET BREAKING SILENCE

Too wearily had we and song
Been left to look and left to long,
Yea, song and we to long and look,
Since thine acquainted feet forsook
The mountain where the Muses hymn
For Sinai and the Seraphim.
Now in both the mountains' shine
Dress thy countenance, twice divine!
From Moses and the Muses draw
The Tables of thy double Law!
His rod-born fount and Castaly
Let the one rock bring forth for thee,
Renewing so from either spring
The songs which both thy countries sing:
Or we shall fear lest, heavened thus long,
Thou should'st forget thy native song,
And mar thy mortal melodies
With broken stammer of the skies.

Ah! let the sweet birds of the Lord
With earth's waters make accord;
Teach how the crucifix may be
Carven from the laurel-tree,
Fruit of the Hesperides
Burnish take on Eden-trees,
The Muses' sacred grove be wet
With the red dew of Olivet,
And Sappho lay her burning brows
In white Cecilia's lap of snows!

Thy childhood must have felt the stings
Of too divine o'ershadowings;
Its odorous heart have been a blossom
That in darkness did unbosom,
Those fire-flies of God to invite,
Burning spirits, which by night
Bear upon their laden wing
To such hearts impregnating.
For flowers that night-wings fertilize
Mock down the stars' unsteady eyes,
And with a happy, sleepless glance
Gaze the moon out of countenance.
I think thy girlhood's watchers must

Have took thy folded songs on trust,
And felt them, as one feels the stir
Of still lightnings in the hair,
When conscious hush expects the cloud
To speak the golden secret loud
Which tacit air is privy to;
Flasked in the grape the wine they knew,
Ere thy poet-mouth was able
For its first young starry babble.
Keep'st thou not yet that subtle grace?
Yea, in this silent interspace,
God sets His poems in thy face!

The loom which mortal verse affords,
Out of weak and mortal words,
Wovest thou thy singing-weed in,
To a rune of thy far Eden.
Vain are all disguises! Ah,
Heavenly incognita!
Thy mien bewrayeth through that wrong
The great Uranian House of Song!
As the vintages of earth
Taste of the sun that riped their birth,
We know what never cadent Sun
Thy lamped clusters throbbed upon,
What plumed feet the winepress trod;
Thy wine is flavorous of God.
Whatever singing-robe thou wear
Has the Paradisal air;
And some gold feather it has kept
Shows what Floor it lately swept!

"MANUS ANIMAM PINXIT"

Lady who hold'st on me dominion!
Within your spirit's arms I stay me fast
Against the fell
Immitigate ravening of the gates of hell;
And claim my right in you, most hardly won,
Of chaste fidelity upon the chaste:
Hold me and hold by me, lest both should fall
(O in high escalade high companion!)
Even in the breach of Heaven's assaulted wall.
Like to a wind-sown sapling grow I from
The clift, Sweet, of your skyward-jetting soul, -
Shook by all gusts that sweep it, overcome
By all its clouds incumbent: O be true
To your soul, dearest, as my life to you!
For if that soil grow sterile, then the whole
Of me must shrivel, from the topmost shoot
Of climbing poesy, and my life, killed through,
Dry down and perish to the foodless root.

Sweet Summer! unto you this swallow drew,
By secret instincts inappeasable,
That did direct him well,
Lured from his gelid North which wrought him wrong,
Wintered of sunning song; -
By happy instincts inappeasable,
Ah yes! that led him well,
Lured to the untried regions and the new
Climes of auspicious you;
To twitter there, and in his singing dwell.
But ah! if you, my Summer, should grow waste,
With grieving skies o'ercast,
For such migration my poor wing was strong
But once; it has no power to fare again
Forth o'er the heads of men,
Nor other Summers for its Sanctuary:
But from your mind's chilled sky
It needs must drop, and lie with stiffened wings
Among your soul's forlornest things;
A speck upon your memory, alack!
A dead fly in a dusty window-crack.

O therefore you who are
What words, being to such mysteries
As raiment to the body is,
Should rather hide than tell;
Chaste and intelligential love:
Whose form is as a grove
Hushed with the cooing of an unseen dove;
Whose spirit to my touch thrills purer far
Than is the tingling of a silver bell;
Whose body other ladies well might bear
As soul,—yea, which it profanation were
For all but you to take as fleshly woof,
Being spirit truest proof;
Whose spirit sure is lineal to that
Which sang Magnificat:
Chastest, since such you are,
Take this curbed spirit of mine,
Which your own eyes invest with light divine,
For lofty love and high auxiliar
In daily exalt emprise
Which outsoars mortal eyes;
This soul which on your soul is laid,
As maid's breast against breast of maid;
Beholding how your own I have engraved
On it, and with what purging thoughts have laved
This love of mine from all mortality
Indeed the copy is a painful one,
And with long labour done!
O if you doubt the thing you are, lady,
Come then, and look in me;
Your beauty, Dian, dress and contemplate
Within a pool to Dian consecrate!
Unveil this spirit, lady, when you will,
For unto all but you 'tis veiled still:
Unveil, and fearless gaze there, you alone,
And if you love the image—'tis your own!

A CARRIER SONG

I.

    Since you have waned from us,
    Fairest of women!
    I am a darkened cage
    Song cannot hymn in.
    My songs have followed you,
    Like birds the summer;
    Ah! bring them back to me,
    Swiftly, dear comer!
    Seraphim,
    Her to hymn,
    Might leave their portals;
    And at my feet learn
    The harping of mortals!

II.

    Where wings to rustle use,
    But this poor tarrier -
    Searching my spirit's eaves -
    Find I for carrier.
    Ah! bring them back to me
    Swiftly, sweet comer!
    Swift, swift, and bring with you
    Song's Indian summer!
    Seraphim,
    Her to hymn,
    Might leave their portals;
    And at my feet learn
    The harping of mortals!

III.

    Whereso your angel is,
    My angel goeth;
    I am left guardianless,
    Paradise knoweth!
    I have no Heaven left
    To weep my wrongs to;
    Heaven, when you went from us;
    Went with my songs too.
    Seraphim,
    Her to hymn,
    Might leave their portals;
    And at my feet learn

The harping of mortals!

IV.
    I have no angels left
    Now, Sweet, to pray to:
    Where you have made your shrine
    They are away to.
    They have struck Heaven's tent,
    And gone to cover you:
    Whereso you keep your state
    Heaven is pitched over you!
    Seraphim,
    Her to hymn,
    Might leave their portals;
    And at my feet learn
    The harping of mortals!

V.
    She that is Heaven's Queen
    Her title borrows,
    For that she pitiful
    Beareth our sorrows.
    So thou, Regina mi,
    Spes infirmorum;
    With all our grieving crowned
    Mater dolorum!
    Seraphim,
    Her to hymn,
    Might leave their portals;
    And at my feet learn
    The harping of mortals!

VI.
    Yet, envious coveter
    Of other's grieving!
    This lonely longing yet
    'Scapeth your reaving.
    Cruel! to take from a
    Sinner his Heaven!
    Think you with contrite smiles
    To be forgiven?
    Seraphim,
    Her to hymn,
    Might leave their portals;
    And at my feet learn

The harping of mortals!

VII.
Penitent! give me back
Angels, and Heaven;
Render your stolen self,
And be forgiven!
How frontier Heaven from you?
For my soul prays, Sweet,
Still to your face in Heaven,
Heaven in your face, Sweet!
Seraphim,
Her to hymn,
Might leave their portals;
And at my feet learn
The harping of mortals!

SCALA JACOBI PORTAQUE EBURNEA

Her soul from earth to Heaven lies,
Like the ladder of the vision,
Whereon go
To and fro,
In ascension and demission,
Star-flecked feet of Paradise.

Now she is drawn up from me,
All my angels, wet-eyed, tristful,
Gaze from great
Heaven's gate
Like pent children, very wistful,
That below a playmate see.

Dream-dispensing face of hers!
Ivory port which loosed upon me
Wings, I wist,
Whose amethyst
Trepidations have forgone me, -
Hesper's filmy traffickers!

GILDED GOLD

Thou dost to rich attire a grace,
To let it deck itself with thee,
And teachest pomp strange cunning ways
To be thought simplicity.
But lilies, stolen from grassy mold,
No more curled state unfold
Translated to a vase of gold;
In burning throne though they keep still
Serenities unthawed and chill.
Therefore, albeit thou'rt stately so,
In statelier state thou us'dst to go.

Though jewels should phosphoric burn
Through those night-waters of thine hair,
A flower from its translucid urn
Poured silver flame more lunar-fair.
These futile trappings but recall
Degenerate worshippers who fall
In purfled kirtle and brocade
To 'parel the white Mother-Maid.
For, as her image stood arrayed
In vests of its self-substance wrought

To measure of the sculptor's thought -
Slurred by those added braveries;
So for thy spirit did devise
Its Maker seemly garniture,
Of its own essence parcel pure, -
From grave simplicities a dress,
And reticent demurenesses,
And love encinctured with reserve;
Which the woven vesture should subserve.
For outward robes in their ostents
Should show the soul's habiliments.
Therefore I say,—Thou'rt fair even so,
But better Fair I use to know.

The violet would thy dusk hair deck
With graces like thine own unsought.
Ah! but such place would daze and wreck
Its simple, lowly rustic thought.
For so advanced, dear, to thee,
It would unlearn humility!

Yet do not, with an altered look,
In these weak numbers read rebuke;
Which are but jealous lest too much
God's master-piece thou shouldst retouch.
Where a sweetness is complete,
Add not sweets unto the sweet!
Or, as thou wilt, for others so
In unfamiliar richness go;
But keep for mine acquainted eyes
The fashions of thy Paradise.

HER PORTRAIT

Oh, but the heavenly grammar did I hold
Of that high speech which angels' tongues turn gold!
So should her deathless beauty take no wrong,
Praised in her own great kindred's fit and cognate tongue.
Or if that language yet with us abode.
Which Adam in the garden talked with God!
But our untempered speech descends—poor heirs!
Grimy and rough-cast still from Babel's bricklayers:
Curse on the brutish jargon we inherit,
Strong but to damn, not memorise, a spirit!
A cheek, a lip, a limb, a bosom, they
Move with light ease in speech of working-day;
And women we do use to praise even so.
But here the gates we burst, and to the temple go.
Their praise were her dispraise; who dare, who dare,
Adulate the seraphim for their burning hair?
How, if with them I dared, here should I dare it?
How praise the woman, who but know the spirit?
How praise the colour of her eyes, uncaught
While they were coloured with her varying thought
How her mouth's shape, who only use to know
What tender shape her speech will fit it to?
Or her lips' redness, when their joined veil
Song's fervid hand has parted till it wore them pale?

If I would praise her soul (temerarious if!),
All must be mystery and hieroglyph.
Heaven, which not oft is prodigal of its more
To singers, in their song too great before;
By which the hierarch of large poesy is
Restrained to his once sacred benefice;
Only for her the salutary awe
Relaxes and stern canon of its law;
To her alone concedes pluralities,
In her alone to reconcile agrees
The Muse, the Graces, and the Charities;
To her, who can the trust so well conduct
To her it gives the use, to us the usufruct.

What of the dear administress then may
I utter, though I spoke her own carved perfect way?
What of her daily gracious converse known,
Whose heavenly despotism must needs dethrone

And subjugate all sweetness but its own?
Deep in my heart subsides the infrequent word,
And there dies slowly throbbing like a wounded bird.
What of her silence, that outsweetens speech?
What of her thoughts, high marks for mine own thoughts to reach?
Yet (Chaucer's antique sentence so to turn),
Most gladly will she teach, and gladly learn;
And teaching her, by her enchanting art,
The master threefold learns for all he can impart.
Now all is said, and all being said,—aye me!
There yet remains unsaid the very She.
Nay, to conclude (so to conclude I dare),
If of her virtues you evade the snare,
Then for her faults you'll fall in love with her.

Alas, and I have spoken of her Muse -
Her Muse, that died with her auroral dews!
Learn, the wise cherubim from harps of gold
Seduce a trepidating music manifold;
But the superior seraphim do know
None other music but to flame and glow.
So she first lighted on our frosty earth,
A sad musician, of cherubic birth,
Playing to alien ears—which did not prize
The uncomprehended music of the skies -
The exiled airs of her far Paradise.
But soon from her own harpings taking fire,
In love and light her melodies expire.
Now Heaven affords her, for her silenced hymn,
A double portion of the seraphim.

At the rich odours from her heart that rise,
My soul remembers its lost Paradise,
And antenatal gales blow from Heaven's shores of spice;
I grow essential all, uncloaking me
From this encumbering virility,
And feel the primal sex of heaven and poetry:
And parting from her, in me linger on
Vague snatches of Uranian antiphon.

How to the petty prison could she shrink
Of femineity?—Nay, but I think
In a dear courtesy her spirit would
Woman assume, for grace to womanhood.
Or, votaress to the virgin Sanctitude

Of reticent withdrawal's sweet, courted pale,
She took the cloistral flesh, the sexual veil,
Of her sad, aboriginal sisterhood;
The habit of cloistral flesh which founding Eve indued.

Thus do I know her: but for what men call
Beauty—the loveliness corporeal,
Its most just praise a thing unproper were
To singer or to listener, me or her.
She wears that body but as one indues
A robe, half careless, for it is the use;
Although her soul and it so fair agree,
We sure may, unattaint of heresy,
Conceit it might the soul's begetter be.
The immortal could we cease to contemplate,
The mortal part suggests its every trait.
God laid His fingers on the ivories
Of her pure members as on smoothed keys,
And there out-breathed her spirit's harmonies
I'll speak a little proudly:- I disdain
To count the beauty worth my wish or gaze,
Which the dull daily fool can covet or obtain.
I do confess the fairness of the spoil,
But from such rivalry it takes a soil.
For her I'll proudlier speak:- how could it be
That I should praise the gilding on the psaltery?
'Tis not for her to hold that prize a prize,
Or praise much praise, though proudest in its wise,
To which even hopes of merely women rise.
Such strife would to the vanquished laurels yield,
Against HER suffered to have lost a field.
Herself must with herself be sole compeer,
Unless the people of her distant sphere
Some gold migration send to melodise the year.
But first our hearts must burn in larger guise,
To reformate the uncharitable skies,
And so the deathless plumage to acclimatise:
Since this, their sole congener in our clime,
Droops her sad, ruffled thoughts for half the shivering time.

Yet I have felt what terrors may consort
In women's cheeks, the Graces' soft resort;
My hand hath shook at gentle hands' access,
And trembled at the waving of a tress;
My blood known panic fear, and fled dismayed,

Where ladies' eyes have set their ambuscade.
The rustle of a robe hath been to me
The very rattle of love's musketry;
Although my heart hath beat the loud advance,
I have recoiled before a challenging glance,
Proved gay alarms where warlike ribbons dance.
And from it all, this knowledge have I got, -
The whole that others have, is less than they have not;
All which makes other women noted fair,
Unnoted would remain and overshone in her.

How should I gauge what beauty is her dole,
Who cannot see her countenance for her soul;
As birds see not the casement for the sky?
And as 'tis check they prove its presence by,
I know not of her body till I find
My flight debarred the heaven of her mind.
Hers is the face whence all should copied be,
Did God make replicas of such as she;
Its presence felt by what it does abate,
Because the soul shines through tempered and mitigate:
Where—as a figure labouring at night
Beside the body of a splendid light -
Dark Time works hidden by its luminousness;
And every line he labours to impress
Turns added beauty, like the veins that run
Athwart a leaf which hangs against the sun.

There regent Melancholy wide controls;
There Earth- and Heaven-Love play for aureoles;
There Sweetness out of Sadness breaks at fits,
Like bubbles on dark water, or as flits
A sudden silver fin through its deep infinites;
There amorous Thought has sucked pale Fancy's breath,
And Tenderness sits looking toward the lands of death
There Feeling stills her breathing with her hand,
And Dream from Melancholy part wrests the wand
And on this lady's heart, looked you so deep,
Poor Poetry has rocked himself to sleep:
Upon the heavy blossom of her lips
Hangs the bee Musing; nigh her lids eclipse
Each half-occulted star beneath that lies;
And in the contemplation of those eyes,
Passionless passion, wild tranquillities.

EPILOGUE—TO THE POET'S SITTER,

Wherein he excuseth himself for the manner of the Portrait.

    Alas! now wilt thou chide, and say (I deem),
    My figured descant hides the simple theme:
    Or in another wise reproving, say
    I ill observe thine own high reticent way.
    Oh, pardon, that I testify of thee
    What thou couldst never speak, nor others be!

    Yet (for the book is not more innocent
    Of what the gazer's eyes makes so intent),
    She will but smile, perhaps, that I find my fair
    Sufficing scope in such strait theme as her.
    "Bird of the sun! the stars' wild honey-bee!
    Is your gold browsing done so thoroughly?
    Or sinks a singed wing to narrow nest in me?"
    (Thus she might say: for not this lowly vein
    Out-deprecates her deprecating strain.)
    Oh, you mistake, dear lady, quite; nor know
    Ether was strict as you, its loftiness as low!

    The heavens do not advance their majesty
    Over their marge; beyond his empery
    The ensigns of the wind are not unfurled,
    His reign is hooped in by the pale o' the world.
    'Tis not the continent, but the contained,
    That pleasaunce makes or prison, loose or chained.
    Too much alike or little captives me,
    For all oppression is captivity.
    What groweth to its height demands no higher;
    The limit limits not, but the desire.
    Give but my spirit its desired scope, -
    A giant in a pismire, I not grope;
    Deny it,—and an ant, with on my back
    A firmament, the skiey vault will crack.
    Our minds make their own Termini, nor call
    The issuing circumscriptions great or small;
    So high constructing Nature lessons to us all:
    Who optics gives accommodate to see
    Your countenance large as looks the sun to be,
    And distant greatness less than near humanity.

We, therefore, with a sure instinctive mind,
An equal spaciousness of bondage find
In confines far or near, of air or our own kind.
Our looks and longings, which affront the stars,
Most richly bruised against their golden bars,
Delighted captives of their flaming spears,
Find a restraint restrainless which appears
As that is, and so simply natural,
In you;—the fair detention freedom call,
And overscroll with fancies the loved prison-wall.

Such sweet captivity, and only such,
In you, as in those golden bars, we touch!
Our gazes for sufficing limits know
The firmament above, your face below;
Our longings are contented with the skies,
Contented with the heaven, and your eyes.
My restless wings, that beat the whole world through,
Flag on the confines of the sun and you;
And find the human pale remoter of the two.

TO THE DEAD CARDINAL OF WESTMINSTER

I will not perturbate
Thy Paradisal state
With praise
Of thy dead days;

To the new-heavened say, -
"Spirit, thou wert fine clay:"
This do,
Thy praise who knew.

Therefore my spirit clings
Heaven's porter by the wings,
And holds
Its gated golds

Apart, with thee to press
A private business; -
Whence,
Deign me audience.

Anchorite, who didst dwell
With all the world for cell
My soul
Round me doth roll

A sequestration bare.
Too far alike we were,
Too far
Dissimilar.

For its burning fruitage I
Do climb the tree o' the sky;
Do prize
Some human eyes.

YOU smelt the Heaven-blossoms,
And all the sweet embosoms
The dear
Uranian year.

Those Eyes my weak gaze shuns,
Which to the suns are Suns.
Did
Not affray your lid.

The carpet was let down
(With golden mouldings strown)
For you
Of the angels' blue.

But I, ex-Paradised,
The shoulder of your Christ
Find high
To lean thereby.

So flaps my helpless sail,
Bellying with neither gale,
Of Heaven
Nor Orcus even.

Life is a coquetry
Of Death, which wearies me,
Too sure
Of the amour;

A tiring-room where I
Death's divers garments try,
Till fit
Some fashion sit.

It seemeth me too much
I do rehearse for such
A mean
And single scene.

The sandy glass hence bear -
Antique remembrancer;
My veins
Do spare its pains.

With secret sympathy
My thoughts repeat in me
Infirm
The turn o' the worm

Beneath my appointed sod:
The grave is in my blood;
I shake
To winds that take

Its grasses by the top;
The rains thereon that drop
Perturb
With drip acerb

My subtly answering soul;
The feet across its knoll
Do jar
Me from afar.

As sap foretastes the spring;
As Earth ere blossoming
Thrills
With far daffodils,

And feels her breast turn sweet
With the unconceived wheat;
So doth
My flesh foreloathe

The abhorred spring of Dis,
With seething presciences
Affirm
The preparate worm.

I have no thought that I,
When at the last I die,
Shall reach
To gain your speech.

But you, should that be so,
May very well, I know,
May well
To me in hell

With recognising eyes
Look from your Paradise -
"God bless
Thy hopelessness!"

Call, holy soul, O call
The hosts angelical,
And say, -
"See, far away

"Lies one I saw on earth;
One stricken from his birth
With curse
Of destinate verse.

"What place doth He ye serve
For such sad spirit reserve, -
Given,
In dark lieu of Heaven,

"The impitiable Daemon,
Beauty, to adore and dream on,
To be
Perpetually

"Hers, but she never his?
He reapeth miseries,
Foreknows
His wages woes;

"He lives detached days;
He serveth not for praise;
For gold
He is not sold;

"Deaf is he to world's tongue;
He scorneth for his song
The loud
Shouts of the crowd;

"He asketh not world's eyes;
Not to world's ears he cries;
Saith,—'These
Shut, if ye please;'

"He measureth world's pleasure,
World's ease as Saints might measure;
For hire
Just love entire

"He asks, not grudging pain;
And knows his asking vain,
And cries -
'Love! Love!' and dies;

"In guerdon of long duty,
Unowned by Love or Beauty;
And goes -
Tell, tell, who knows!

"Aliens from Heaven's worth,
Fine beasts who nose i' the earth,
Do there
Reward prepare.

"But are HIS great desires
Food but for nether fires?
Ah me,
A mystery!

"Can it be his alone,
To find when all is known,
That what
He solely sought

"Is lost, and thereto lost
All that its seeking cost?
That he
Must finally,

"Through sacrificial tears,
And anchoretic years,
Tryst
With the sensualist?"

So ask; and if they tell
The secret terrible,
Good friend,
I pray thee send

Some high gold embassage
To teach my unripe age.
Tell!
Lest my feet walk hell.

A FALLEN YEW

It seemed corrival of the world's great prime,
Made to un-edge the scythe of Time,
And last with stateliest rhyme.

No tender Dryad ever did indue
That rigid chiton of rough yew,
To fret her white flesh through:

But some god like to those grim Asgard lords,
Who walk the fables of the hordes
From Scandinavian fjords,

Upheaved its stubborn girth, and raised unriven,
Against the whirl-blast and the levin,
Defiant arms to Heaven.

When doom puffed out the stars, we might have said,
It would decline its heavy head,
And see the world to bed.

For this firm yew did from the vassal leas,
And rain and air, its tributaries,
Its revenues increase,

And levy impost on the golden sun,
Take the blind years as they might run,
And no fate seek or shun.

But now our yew is strook, is fallen—yea
Hacked like dull wood of every day
To this and that, men say.

Never! -To Hades' shadowy shipyards gone,
Dim barge of Dis, down Acheron
It drops, or Lethe wan.

Stirred by its fall—poor destined bark of Dis! -
Along my soul a bruit there is
Of echoing images,

Reverberations of mortality:
Spelt backward from its death, to me
Its life reads saddenedly.

Its breast was hollowed as the tooth of eld;
And boys, their creeping unbeheld,
A laughing moment dwelled.

Yet they, within its very heart so crept,
Reached not the heart that courage kept
With winds and years beswept.

And in its boughs did close and kindly nest
The birds, as they within its breast,
By all its leaves caressed.

But bird nor child might touch by any art
Each other's or the tree's hid heart,
A whole God's breadth apart;

The breadth of God, he breadth of death and life!
Even so, even so, in undreamed strife
With pulseless Law, the wife, -

The sweetest wife on sweetest marriage-day, -
Their souls at grapple in mid-way,
Sweet to her sweet may say:

"I take you to my inmost heart, my true!"
Ah, fool! but there is one heart you
Shall never take him to!

The hold that falls not when the town is got,
The heart's heart, whose immured plot
Hath keys yourself keep not!

Its ports you cannot burst—you are withstood -
For him that to your listening blood
Sends precepts as he would.

Its gates are deaf to Love, high summoner;
Yea, Love's great warrant runs not there:
You are your prisoner.

Yourself are with yourself the sole consortress
In that unleaguerable fortress;
It knows you not for portress

Its keys are at the cincture hung of God;

Its gates are trepidant to His nod;
By Him its floors are trod.

And if His feet shall rock those floors in wrath,
Or blest aspersion sleek His path,
Is only choice it hath.

Yea, in that ultimate heart's occult abode
To lie as in an oubliette of God,
Or as a bower untrod,

Built by a secret Lover for His Spouse; -
Sole choice is this your life allows,
Sad tree, whose perishing boughs
So few birds house!

DREAM-TRYST

The breaths of kissing night and day
Were mingled in the eastern Heaven:
Throbbing with unheard melody
Shook Lyra all its star-chord seven:
When dusk shrunk cold, and light trod shy,
And dawn's grey eyes were troubled grey;
And souls went palely up the sky,
And mine to Lucide.

There was no change in her sweet eyes
Since last I saw those sweet eyes shine;
There was no change in her deep heart
Since last that deep heart knocked at mine.
Her eyes were clear, her eyes were Hope's,
Wherein did ever come and go
The sparkle of the fountain-drops
From her sweet soul below.

The chambers in the house of dreams
Are fed with so divine an air,
That Time's hoar wings grow young therein,
And they who walk there are most fair.
I joyed for me, I joyed for her,
Who with the Past meet girt about:
Where our last kiss still warms the air,
Nor can her eyes go out.

A CORYMBUS FOR AUTUMN

Hearken my chant, 'tis
As a Bacchante's,
A grape-spurt, a vine-splash, a tossed tress, flown vaunt 'tis!
Suffer my singing,
Gipsy of Seasons, ere thou go winging;
Ere Winter throws
His slaking snows
In thy feasting-flagon's impurpurate glows!
The sopped sun—toper as ever drank hard -
Stares foolish, hazed,
Rubicund, dazed,
Totty with thine October tankard.
Tanned maiden! with cheeks like apples russet,
And breast a brown agaric faint-flushing at tip,
And a mouth too red for the moon to buss it,
But her cheek unvow its vestalship;
Thy mists enclip
Her steel-clear circuit illuminous,
Until it crust
Rubiginous
With the glorious gules of a glowing rust.
Far other saw we, other indeed,
The crescent moon, in the May-days dead,
Fly up with its slender white wings spread
Out of its nest in the sea's waved mead!
How are the veins of thee, Autumn, laden?
Umbered juices,
And pulped oozes
Pappy out of the cherry-bruises,
Froth the veins of thee, wild, wild maiden!
With hair that musters
In globed clusters,
In tumbling clusters, like swarthy grapes,
Round thy brow and thine ears o'ershaden;
With the burning darkness of eyes like pansies,
Like velvet pansies
Wherethrough escapes
The splendid might of thy conflagrate fancies;
With robe gold-tawny not hiding the shapes
Of the feet whereunto it falleth down,
Thy naked feet unsandalled;
With robe gold-tawny that does not veil
Feet where the red

Is meshed in the brown,
Like a rubied sun in a Venice-sail.

The wassailous heart of the Year is thine!
His Bacchic fingers disentwine
His coronal
At thy festival;
His revelling fingers disentwine
Leaf, flower, and all,
And let them fall
Blossom and all in thy wavering wine.
The Summer looks out from her brazen tower,
Through the flashing bars of July,
Waiting thy ripened golden shower;
Whereof there cometh, with sandals fleet,
The North-west flying viewlessly,
With a sword to sheer, and untameable feet,
And the gorgon-head of the Winter shown
To stiffen the gazing earth as stone.

In crystal Heaven's magic sphere
Poised in the palm of thy fervid hand,
Thou seest the enchanted shows appear
That stain Favonian firmament;
Richer than ever the Occident
Gave up to bygone Summer's wand.
Day's dying dragon lies drooping his crest,
Panting red pants into the West.
Or the butterfly sunset claps its wings
With flitter alit on the swinging blossom,
The gusty blossom, that tosses and swings,
Of the sea with its blown and ruffled bosom;
Its ruffled bosom wherethrough the wind sings
Till the crisped petals are loosened and strown
Overblown, on the sand;
Shed, curling as dead
Rose-leaves curl, on the flecked strand.
Or higher, holier, saintlier when, as now,
All nature sacerdotal seems, and thou.
The calm hour strikes on yon golden gong,
In tones of floating and mellow light
A spreading summons to even-song:
See how there
The cowled night
Kneels on the Eastern sanctuary-stair.

What is this feel of incense everywhere?
Clings it round folds of the blanch-amiced clouds,
Upwafted by the solemn thurifer,
The mighty spirit unknown,
That swingeth the slow earth before the embannered Throne?
Or is't the Season under all these shrouds
Of light, and sense, and silence, makes her known
A presence everywhere,
An inarticulate prayer,
A hand on the soothed tresses of the air?
But there is one hour scant
Of this Titanian, primal liturgy;
As there is but one hour for me and thee,
Autumn, for thee and thine hierophant,
Of this grave ending chant.
Round the earth still and stark
Heaven's death-lights kindle, yellow spark by spark,
Beneath the dreadful catafalque of the dark.

And I had ended there:
But a great wind blew all the stars to flare,
And cried, "I sweep the path before the moon!
Tarry ye now the coming of the moon,
For she is coming soon;"
Then died before the coming of the moon.
And she came forth upon the trepidant air,
In vesture unimagined-fair,
Woven as woof of flag-lilies;
And curdled as of flag-lilies
The vapour at the feet of her,
And a haze about her tinged in fainter wise.
As if she had trodden the stars in press,
Till the gold wine spurted over her dress,
Till the gold wine gushed out round her feet;
Spouted over her stained wear,
And bubbled in golden froth at her feet,
And hung like a whirlpool's mist round her.
Still, mighty Season, do I see't,
Thy sway is still majestical!
Thou hold'st of God, by title sure,
Thine indefeasible investiture,
And that right round thy locks are native to;
The heavens upon thy brow imperial,
This huge terrene thy ball,

And o'er thy shoulders thrown wide air's depending pall.
What if thine earth be blear and bleak of hue?
Still, still the skies are sweet!
Still, Season, still thou hast thy triumphs there!
How have I, unaware,
Forgetful of my strain inaugural,
Cleft the great rondure of thy reign complete,
Yielding thee half, who hast indeed the all?
I will not think thy sovereignty begun
But with the shepherd sun
That washes in the sea the stars' gold fleeces
Or that with day it ceases,
Who sets his burning lips to the salt brine,
And purples it to wine;
While I behold how ermined Artemis
Ordained weed must wear,
And toil thy business;
Who witness am of her,
Her too in autumn turned a vintager;
And, laden with its lamped clusters bright,
The fiery-fruited vineyard of this night.

THE HOUND OF HEAVEN

I fled Him, down the nights and down the days;
I fled Him, down the arches of the years;
I fled Him, down the labyrinthine ways
Of my own mind; and in the mist of tears
I hid from Him, and under running laughter.
Up vistaed hopes, I sped;
And shot, precipitated
Adown Titanic glooms of chasmed fears,
From those strong Feet that followed, followed after.
But with unhurrying chase,
And unperturbed pace,
Deliberate speed, majestic instancy,
They beat—and a Voice beat
More instant than the Feet -
"All things betray thee, who betrayest Me."

I pleaded, outlaw-wise,
By many a hearted casement, curtained red,
Trellised with intertwining charities;
(For, though I knew His love Who followed,
Yet was I sore adread
Lest, having Him, I must have naught beside)
But, if one little casement parted wide,
The gust of His approach would clash it to
Fear wist not to evade, as Love wist to pursue.
Across the margent of the world I fled,
And troubled the gold gateways of the stars,
Smiting for shelter on their changed bars;
Fretted to dulcet jars
And silvern chatter the pale ports o' the moon.
I said to dawn: Be sudden—to eve: Be soon;
With thy young skiey blossoms heap me over
From this tremendous Lover!
Float thy vague veil about me, lest He see!
I tempted all His servitors, but to find
My own betrayal in their constancy,
In faith to Him their fickleness to me,
Their traitorous trueness, and their loyal deceit.
To all swift things for swiftness did I sue;
Clung to the whistling mane of every wind.
But whether they swept, smoothly fleet,
The long savannahs of the blue;
Or whether, Thunder-driven,

They clanged his chariot 'thwart a heaven,
Plashy with flying lightnings round the spurn o' their feet:-
Fear wist not to evade as Love wist to pursue.
Still with unhurrying chase,
And unperturbed pace,
Deliberate speed, majestic instancy,
Came on the following Feet,
And a Voice above their beat -
"Naught shelters thee, who wilt not shelter Me."

I sought no more that, after which I strayed,
In face of man or maid;
But still within the little children's eyes
Seems something, something that replies,
THEY at least are for me, surely for me!
I turned me to them very wistfully;
But just as their young eyes grew sudden fair
With dawning answers there,
Their angel plucked them from me by the hair.
"Come then, ye other children, Nature's—share
With me" (said I) "your delicate fellowship;
Let me greet you lip to lip,
Let me twine with you caresses,
Wantoning
With our Lady-Mother's vagrant tresses,
Banqueting
With her in her wind-walled palace,
Underneath her azured dais,
Quaffing, as your taintless way is,
From a chalice
Lucent-weeping out of the dayspring.'
So it was done:
I in their delicate fellowship was one -
Drew the bolt of Nature's secrecies.
I knew all the swift importings
On the wilful face of skies;
I knew how the clouds arise
Spumed of the wild sea-snortings;
All that's born or dies
Rose and drooped with—made them shapers
Of mine own moods, or wailful or divine -
With them joyed and was bereaven.
I was heavy with the even,
When she lit her glimmering tapers
Round the day's dead sanctities.

I laughed in the morning's eyes.
I triumphed and I saddened with all weather,
Heaven and I wept together,
And its sweet tears were salt with mortal mine;
Against the red throb of its sunset-heart
I laid my own to beat,
And share commingling heat;
But not by that, by that, was eased my human smart.
In vain my tears were wet on Heaven's grey cheek.
For ah! we know not what each other says,
These things and I; in sound I speak -
THEIR sound is but their stir, they speak by silences.
Nature, poor stepdame, cannot slake my drouth;
Let her, if she would owe me,
Drop yon blue bosom-veil of sky, and show me
The breasts o' her tenderness:
Never did any milk of hers once bless
My thirsting mouth.
Nigh and nigh draws the chase,
With unperturbed pace,
Deliberate speed majestic instancy
And past those noised Feet
A voice comes yet more fleet -
"Lo! naught contents thee, who content'st not Me."

Naked I wait Thy love's uplifted stroke!
My harness piece by piece Thou hast hewn from me,
And smitten me to my knee;
I am defenceless utterly,
I slept, methinks, and woke,
And, slowly gazing, find me stripped in sleep.
In the rash lustihead of my young powers,
I shook the pillaring hours
And pulled my life upon me; grimed with smears,
I stand amid the dust o' the mounded years -
My mangled youth lies dead beneath the heap.
My days have crackled and gone up in smoke,
Have puffed and burst as sun-starts on a stream.
Yea, faileth now even dream
The dreamer, and the lute the lutanist;
Even the linked fantasies, in whose blossomy twist
I swung the earth a trinket at my wrist,
Are yielding; cords of all too weak account
For earth with heavy griefs so overplussed.
Ah! is Thy love indeed

A weed, albeit an amaranthine weed,
Suffering no flowers except its own to mount?
Ah! must -
Designer infinite! -
Ah! must Thou char the wood ere Thou canst limn with it?
My freshness spent its wavering shower i' the dust;
And now my heart is as a broken fount,
Wherein tear-drippings stagnate, spilt down ever
From the dank thoughts that shiver
Upon the sighful branches of my mind.
Such is; what is to be?
The pulp so bitter, how shall taste the rind?
I dimly guess what Time in mists confounds;
Yet ever and anon a trumpet sounds
From the hid battlements of Eternity,
Those shaken mists a space unsettle, then
Round the half-glimpsed turrets slowly wash again;
But not ere him who summoneth
I first have seen, enwound
With grooming robes purpureal, cypress-crowned;
His name I know, and what his trumpet saith.
Whether man's heart or life it be which yields
Thee harvest, must Thy harvest fields
Be dunged with rotten death?
Now of that long pursuit
Comes on at hand the bruit;
That Voice is round me like a bursting sea:
"And is thy earth so marred,
Shattered in shard on shard?
Lo, all things fly thee, for thou fliest Me!

"Strange, piteous, futile thing!
Wherefore should any set thee love apart?
Seeing none but I makes much of naught" (He said),
"And human love needs human meriting:
How hast thou merited -
Of all man's clotted clay the dingiest clot?
Alack, thou knowest not
How little worthy of any love thou art!
Whom wilt thou find to love ignoble thee,
Save Me, save only Me?
All which I took from thee I did but take,
Not for thy harms,
But just that thou might'st seek it in My arms.
All which thy child's mistake

Fancies as lost, I have stored for thee at home:
Rise, clasp My hand, and come."

Halts by me that footfall:
Is my gloom, after all,
Shade of His hand, outstretched caressingly?
"Ah, fondest, blindest, weakest,
I am He Whom thou seekest!
Thou dravest love from thee, who dravest Me."

A JUDGMENT IN HEAVEN[1]

Athwart the sod which is treading for God * the poet
    paced with his splendid eyes;
Paradise-verdure he stately passes * to win to the Father of Paradise,
Through the conscious and palpitant grasses * of inter-tangled
    relucent dyes.

The angels a-play on its fields of Summer * (their wild wings rustled
    his guides' cymars)
Looked up from disport at the passing comer, * as they pelted each
    other with handfuls of stars;
And the warden-spirits with startled feet rose, * hand on sword, by
    their tethered cars.

With plumes night-tinctured englobed and cinctured, * of Saints, his
    guided steps held on
To where on the far crystelline pale * of that transtellar Heaven
    there shone
The immutable crocean dawn * effusing from the Father's Throne.

Through the reverberant Eden-ways * the bruit of his great advent driven,
Back from the fulgent justle and press * with mighty echoing so was given,
As when the surly thunder smites * upon the clanged gates of Heaven.

Over the bickering gonfalons, * far-ranged as for Tartarean wars,
Went a waver of ribbed fire *—as night-seas on phosphoric bars
Like a flame-plumed fan shake slowly out * their ridgy reach
    of crumbling stars.

At length to where on His fretted Throne * sat in the heart of
    His aged dominions
The great Triune, and Mary nigh, * lit round with spears of their
    hauberked minions,
The poet drew, in the thunderous blue * involved dread of those
    mounted pinions.

As in a secret and tenebrous cloud * the watcher from the disquiet earth
At momentary intervals * beholds from its ragged rifts break forth
The flash of a golden perturbation, * the travelling threat of a
    witched birth;

---

[1] I have throughout this poem used an asterisk to indicate the caesura in the middle of the line, after the manner of the old Saxon section-point.

Till heavily parts a sinister chasm, * a grisly jaw, whose verges soon,
Slowly and ominously filled * by the on-coming plenilune,
Supportlessly congest with fire, * and suddenly spit forth the moon:-
With beauty, not terror, through tangled error * of night-dipt
    plumes so burned their charge;
Swayed and parted the globing clusters * so,—disclosed from their
    kindling marge,
Roseal-chapleted, splendent-vestured, * the singer there where
    God's light lay large.

Hu, hu! a wonder! a wonder! see, * clasping the singer's glories clings
A dingy creature, even to laughter * cloaked and clad in patchwork things,
Shrinking close from the unused glows * of the seraphs'
    versicoloured wings.

A rhymer, rhyming a futile rhyme, * he had crept for convoy
    through Eden-ways
Into the shade of the poet's glory, * darkened under his prevalent rays,
Fearfully hoping a distant welcome * as a poor kinsman of his lays.

The angels laughed with a lovely scorning: *—"Who has done this
    sorry deed in
The garden of our Father, God? * 'mid his blossoms to sow this weed in?
Never our fingers knew this stuff: * not so fashion the looms of Eden!"

The singer bowed his brow majestic, * searching that patchwork
    through and through,
Feeling God's lucent gazes traverse * his singing-stoling and spirit too:
The hallowed harpers were fain to frown * on the strange thing
    come 'mid their sacred crew,
Only the singer that was earth * his fellow-earth and his own self knew.

But the poet rent off robe and wreath, * so as a sloughing serpent doth,
Laid them at the rhymer's feet, * shed down wreath and raiment both,
Stood in a dim and shamed stole, * like the tattered wing of a musty moth.

"Thou gav'st the weed and wreath of song, * the weed and wreath
    are solely Thine,
And this dishonest vesture * is the only vesture that is mine;
The life I textured, Thou the song *—MY handicraft is not divine!"

He wrested o'er the rhymer's head * that garmenting which
wrought
    him wrong;
A flickering tissue argentine * down dripped its shivering silvers long:-

"Better thou wov'st thy woof of life * than thou didst weave thy
    woof of song!"

Never a chief in Saintdom was, * but turned him from the Poet then;
Never an eye looked mild on him * 'mid all the angel myriads ten,
Save sinless Mary, and sinful Mary *—the Mary titled Magdalen.

"Turn yon robe," spake Magdalen, * "of torn bright song, and see
    and feel."
They turned the raiment, saw and felt * what their turning did reveal -
All the inner surface piled * with bloodied hairs, like hairs of steel.

"Take, I pray, yon chaplet up, * thrown down ruddied from his head."
They took the roseal chaplet up, * and they stood astonished:
Every leaf between their fingers, * as they bruised it, burst and bled.

"See his torn flesh through those rents; * see the punctures round
    his hair,
As if the chaplet-flowers had driven * deep roots in to nourish there -
Lord, who gav'st him robe and wreath, * WHAT was this Thou
    gav'st for wear?"

"Fetch forth the Paradisal garb!" * spake the Father, sweet and low;
Drew them both by the frightened hand * where Mary's throne
    made irised bow -
"Take, Princess Mary, of thy good grace, * two spirits greater than
    they know."

EPILOGUE

Virtue may unlock hell, or even
A sin turn in the wards of Heaven,
(As ethics of the text-book go),
So little men their own deeds know,
Or through the intricate melee
Guess whitherward draws the battle-sway;
So little, if they know the deed,
Discern what therefrom shall succeed.
To wisest moralists 'tis but given
To work rough border-law of Heaven,
Within this narrow life of ours,
These marches 'twixt delimitless Powers.
Is it, if Heaven the future showed,
Is it the all-severest mode
To see ourselves with the eyes of God?
God rather grant, at His assize,
He see us not with our own eyes!

Heaven, which man's generations draws
Nor deviates into replicas,
Must of as deep diversity
In judgment as creation be.
There is no expeditious road
To pack and label men for God,
And save them by the barrel-load.
Some may perchance, with strange surprise,
Have blundered into Paradise.
In vasty dusk of life abroad,
They fondly thought to err from God,
Nor knew the circle that they trod;
And wandering all the night about,
Found them at morn where they set out.
Death dawned; Heaven lay in prospect wide:-
Lo! they were standing by His side!

The rhymer a life uncomplex,
With just such cares as mortals vex,
So simply felt as all men feel,
Lived purely out to his soul's weal.
A double life the Poet lived,
And with a double burthen grieved;
The life of flesh and life of song,
The pangs to both lives that belong;

Immortal knew and mortal pain,
Who in two worlds could lose and gain.
And found immortal fruits must be
Mortal through his mortality.
The life of flesh and life of song!
If one life worked the other wrong,
What expiating agony
May for him damned to poesy
Shut in that little sentence be -
What deep austerities of strife -
"He lived his life." He lived HIS life!

DAISY

Where the thistle lifts a purple crown
Six foot out of the turf,
And the harebell shakes on the windy hill -
O the breath of the distant surf! -

The hills look over on the South,
And southward dreams the sea;
And, with the sea-breeze hand in hand,
Came innocence and she.

Where 'mid the gorse the raspberry
Red for the gatherer springs,
Two children did we stray and talk
Wise, idle, childish things.

She listened with big-lipped surprise,
Breast-deep mid flower and spine:
Her skin was like a grape, whose veins
Run snow instead of wine.

She knew not those sweet words she spake,
Nor knew her own sweet way;
But there's never a bird, so sweet a song
Thronged in whose throat that day!

Oh, there were flowers in Storrington
On the turf and on the spray;
But the sweetest flower on Sussex hills
Was the Daisy-flower that day!

Her beauty smoothed earth's furrowed face!
She gave me tokens three:-
A look, a word of her winsome mouth,
And a wild raspberry.

A berry red, a guileless look,
A still word,—strings of sand!
And yet they made my wild, wild heart
Fly down to her little hand.

For standing artless as the air,
And candid as the skies,
She took the berries with her hand,
And the love with her sweet eyes.

The fairest things have fleetest end:
Their scent survives their close,
But the rose's scent is bitterness
To him that loved the rose!

She looked a little wistfully,
Then went her sunshine way:-
The sea's eye had a mist on it,
And the leaves fell from the day.

She went her unremembering way,
She went and left in me
The pang of all the partings gone,
And partings yet to be.

She left me marvelling why my soul
Was sad that she was glad;
At all the sadness in the sweet,
The sweetness in the sad.

Still, still I seemed to see her, still
Look up with soft replies,
And take the berries with her hand,
And the love with her lovely eyes.

Nothing begins, and nothing ends,
That is not paid with moan;
For we are born in other's pain,
And perish in our own.

THE MAKING OF VIOLA

I.

    THE FATHER OF HEAVEN.
    Spin, daughter Mary, spin,
    Twirl your wheel with silver din;
    Spin, daughter Mary, spin,
    Spin a tress for Viola.
    ANGELS.
    Spin, Queen Mary, a
    Brown tress for Viola!

II.

    THE FATHER OF HEAVEN.
    Weave, hands angelical,
    Weave a woof of flesh to pall -
    Weave, hands angelical -
    Flesh to pall our Viola.
    ANGELS.
    Weave, singing brothers, a
    Velvet flesh for Viola!

III.

    THE FATHER OF HEAVEN.
    Scoop, young Jesus, for her eyes,
    Wood-browned pools of Paradise -
    Young Jesus, for the eyes,
    For the eyes of Viola.
    ANGELS.
    Tint, Prince Jesus, a
    Dusked eye for Viola!

IV.

    THE FATHER OF HEAVEN.
    Cast a star therein to drown,
    Like a torch in cavern brown,
    Sink a burning star to drown
    Whelmed in eyes of Viola.
    ANGELS.
    Lave, Prince Jesus, a
    Star in eyes of Viola!

V.
    THE FATHER OF HEAVEN.
    Breathe, Lord Paraclete,
    To a bubbled crystal meet -
    Breathe, Lord Paraclete -
    Crystal soul for Viola.
    ANGELS.
    Breathe, Regal Spirit, a
    Flashing soul for Viola!

VI.
    THE FATHER OF HEAVEN.
    Child-angels, from your wings
    Fall the roseal hoverings,
    Child-angels, from your wings,
    On the cheeks of Viola.
    ANGELS.
    Linger, rosy reflex, a
    Quenchless stain, on Viola!

    All things being accomplished, saith the Father of Heaven.
    Bear her down, and bearing, sing,
    Bear her down on spyless wing,
    Bear her down, and bearing, sing,
    With a sound of viola.
    ANGELS.
    Music as her name is, a
    Sweet sound of Viola!

VIII.
    Wheeling angels, past espial,
    Danced her down with sound of viol;
    Wheeling angels, past espial,
    Descanting on "Viola."
    ANGELS.
    Sing, in our footing, a
    Lovely lilt of "Viola!"

IX.
    Baby smiled, mother wailed,
    Earthward while the sweetling sailed;
    Mother smiled, baby wailed,
    When to earth came Viola.
    AND HER ELDERS SHALL SAY:-
    So soon have we taught you a
    Way to weep, poor Viola!

X.
    Smile, sweet baby, smile,
    For you will have weeping-while;
    Native in your Heaven is smile, -
    But your weeping, Viola?

    Whence your smiles we know, but ah?
    Whence your weeping, Viola? -
    Our first gift to you is a
    Gift of tears, my Viola!

TO MY GODCHILD—FRANCIS M. W. M

This labouring, vast, Tellurian galleon,
Riding at anchor off the orient sun,
Had broken its cable, and stood out to space
Down some frore Arctic of the aerial ways:
And now, back warping from the inclement main,
Its vaporous shroudage drenched with icy rain,
It swung into its azure roads again;
When, floated on the prosperous sun-gale, you
Lit, a white halcyon auspice, 'mid our frozen crew.

To the Sun, stranger, surely you belong,
Giver of golden days and golden song;
Nor is it by an all-unhappy plan
You bear the name of me, his constant Magian.
Yet ah! from any other that it came,
Lest fated to my fate you be, as to my name.
When at the first those tidings did they bring,
My heart turned troubled at the ominous thing:
Though well may such a title him endower,
For whom a poet's prayer implores a poet's power.
The Assisian, who kept plighted faith to three,
To Song, to Sanctitude, and Poverty,
(In two alone of whom most singers prove
A fatal faithfulness of during love!);
He the sweet Sales, of whom we scarcely ken
How God he could love more, he so loved men;
The crown and crowned of Laura and Italy;
And Fletcher's fellow—from these, and not from me,
Take you your name, and take your legacy!

Or, if a right successive you declare
When worms, for ivies, intertwine my hair,
Take but this Poesy that now followeth
My clayey hest with sullen servile breath,
Made then your happy freedman by testating death.
My song I do but hold for you in trust,
I ask you but to blossom from my dust.
When you have compassed all weak I began,
Diviner poet, and ah! diviner man;
The man at feud with the perduring child
In you before song's altar nobly reconciled;
From the wise heavens I half shall smile to see
How little a world, which owned you, needed me.

If, while you keep the vigils of the night,
For your wild tears make darkness all too bright,
Some lone orb through your lonely window peeps,
As it played lover over your sweet sleeps;
Think it a golden crevice in the sky,
Which I have pierced but to behold you by!

And when, immortal mortal, droops your head,
And you, the child of deathless song, are dead;
Then, as you search with unaccustomed glance
The ranks of Paradise for my countenance,
Turn not your tread along the Uranian sod
Among the bearded counsellors of God;
For if in Eden as on earth are we,
I sure shall keep a younger company:
Pass where beneath their ranged gonfalons
The starry cohorts shake their shielded suns,
The dreadful mass of their enridged spears;
Pass where majestical the eternal peers,
The stately choice of the great Saintdom, meet -
A silvern segregation, globed complete
In sandalled shadow of the Triune feet;
Pass by where wait, young poet-wayfarer,
Your cousined clusters, emulous to share
With you the roseal lightnings burning 'mid their hair;
Pass the crystalline sea, the Lampads seven:-
Look for me in the nurseries of Heaven.

THE POPPY—TO MONICA

Summer set lip to earth's bosom bare.
And left the flushed print in a poppy there:
Like a yawn of fire from the grass it came,
And the fanning wind puffed it to flapping flame.

With burnt mouth red like a lion's it drank
The blood of the sun as he slaughtered sank,
And dipped its cup in the purpurate shine
When the eastern conduits ran with wine.

Till it grew lethargied with fierce bliss,
And hot as a swinked gipsy is,
And drowsed in sleepy savageries,
With mouth wide a-pout for a sultry kiss.

A child and man paced side by side,
Treading the skirts of eventide;
But between the clasp of his hand and hers
Lay, felt not, twenty withered years.

She turned, with the rout of her dusk South hair,
And saw the sleeping gipsy there;
And snatched and snapped it in swift child's whim,
With—"Keep it, long as you live!"—to him.

And his smile, as nymphs from their laving meres,
Trembled up from a bath of tears;
And joy, like a mew sea-rocked apart,
Tossed on the wave of his troubled heart.

For HE saw what she did not see,
That—as kindled by its own fervency -
The verge shrivelled inward smoulderingly:

And suddenly 'twixt his hand and hers
He knew the twenty withered years -
No flower, but twenty shrivelled years.

"Was never such thing until this hour,"
Low to his heart he said; "the flower
Of sleep brings wakening to me,
And of oblivion memory."

"Was never this thing to me," he said,
"Though with bruised poppies my feet are red!"
And again to his own heart very low:
"O child! I love, for I love and know;

"But you, who love nor know at all
The diverse chambers in Love's guest-hall,
Where some rise early, few sit long:
In how differing accents hear the throng
His great Pentecostal tongue;

"Who know not love from amity,
Nor my reported self from me;
A fair fit gift is this, meseems,
You give—this withering flower of dreams.

"O frankly fickle, and fickly true,
Do you know what the days will do to you?
To your Love and you what the days will do,
O frankly fickle, and fickly true?

"You have loved me, Fair, three lives—or days:
'Twill pass with the passing of my face.
But where I go, your face goes too,
To watch lest I play false to you.

"I am but, my sweet, your foster-lover,
Knowing well when certain years are over
You vanish from me to another;
Yet I know, and love, like the foster-mother.

"So, frankly fickle, and fickly true!
For my brief life—while I take from you
This token, fair and fit, meseems,
For me—this withering flower of dreams."

* * * * *

The sleep-flower sways in the wheat its head,
Heavy with dreams, as that with bread:
The goodly grain and the sun-flushed sleeper
The reaper reaps, and Time the reaper.

I hang 'mid men my needless head,
And my fruit is dreams, as theirs is bread:

The goodly men and the sun-hazed sleeper
Time shall reap, but after the reaper
The world shall glean of me, me the sleeper!

Love! love! your flower of withered dream
In leaved rhyme lies safe, I deem,
Sheltered and shut in a nook of rhyme,
From the reaper man, and his reaper Time.

Love! I fall into the claws of Time:
But lasts within a leaved rhyme
All that the world of me esteems -
My withered dreams, my withered dreams.

TO MONICA THOUGHT DYING

You, O the piteous you!
Who all the long night through
Anticipatedly
Disclose yourself to me
Already in the ways
Beyond our human comfortable days;
How can you deem what Death
Impitiably saith
To me, who listening wake
For your poor sake?
When a grown woman dies
You know we think unceasingly
What things she said, how sweet, how wise;
And these do make our misery.
But you were (you to me
The dead anticipatedly!)
You—eleven years, was't not, or so? -
Were just a child, you know;
And so you never said
Things sweet immeditatably and wise
To interdict from closure my wet eyes:
But foolish things, my dead, my dead!
Little and laughable,
Your age that fitted well.
And was it such things all unmemorable,
Was it such things could make
Me sob all night for your implacable sake?

Yet, as you said to me,
In pretty make-believe of revelry,
So the night long said Death
With his magniloquent breath;
(And that remembered laughter
Which in our daily uses followed after,
Was all untuned to pity and to awe):
"A cup of chocolate,
One farthing is the rate,
You drink it through a straw."

How could I know, how know
Those laughing words when drenched with sobbing so?
Another voice than yours, than yours, he hath!
My dear, was't worth his breath,

His mighty utterance?—yet he saith, and saith!
This dreadful Death to his own dreadfulness
Doth dreadful wrong,
This dreadful childish babble on his tongue!
That iron tongue made to speak sentences,
And wisdom insupportably complete,
Why should it only say the long night through,
In mimicry of you, -
"A cup of chocolate,
One farthing is the rate,
You drink it through a straw, a straw, a straw!"
Oh, of all sentences,
Piercingly incomplete!
Why did you teach that fatal mouth to draw,
Child, impermissible awe,
From your old trivialness?
Why have you done me this
Most unsustainable wrong,
And into Death's control
Betrayed the secret places of my soul?
Teaching him that his lips,
Uttering their native earthquake and eclipse,
Could never so avail
To rend from hem to hem the ultimate veil
Of this most desolate
Spirit, and leave it stripped and desecrate, -
Nay, never so have wrung
From eyes and speech weakness unmanned, unmeet;
As when his terrible dotage to repeat
Its little lesson learneth at your feet;
As when he sits among
His sepulchres, to play
With broken toys your hand has cast away,
With derelict trinkets of the darling young.
Why have you taught—that he might so complete
His awful panoply
From your cast playthings—why,
This dreadful childish babble to his tongue,
Dreadful and sweet?

NEW POEMS

Dedication

Lo, my book thinks to look Time's leaguer down,
Under the banner of your spread renown!
Or if these levies of impuissant rhyme
Fall to the overthrow of assaulting Time,
Yet this one page shall fend oblivious shame,
Armed with your crested and prevailing Name.

Note.—This dedication was written while the dear friend and great oet to whom it was addressed yet lived. It is left as he saw it— he last verses of mine that were ever to pass under his eyes.

F. T.

CONTENTS

SIGHT AND INSIGHT. 1
   The mistress of vision. 1
   Contemplation. 7
   'By reason of Thy law.' 9
   The dread of height. 11
   Orient ode. 14
   New Year's chimes. 19
   From the night of forebeing. 21
   Any saint. 30
   Assumpta Maria. 35
   The after woman. 39
   Grace of the way. 41
   Retrospect. 43

A NARROW VESSEL. 45
   A girl's sin—in her eyes. 45
   A girl's sin—in his eyes. 48
   Love declared. 49
   The way of a maid. 50
   Beginning of the end. 51
   Penelope. 52
   The end of it. 53
   Epilogue. 54

MISCELLANEOUS ODES. 55
   Ode to the setting sun. 55
   After-strain 62
   A captain of song. 64
   Against Urania. 66
   An anthem of earth. 67

MISCELLANEOUS POEMS. 77
   'Ex ore infantium.' 77
   A question. 79
   Field-flower. 81
   The cloud's swan-song. 82
   To the sinking sun. 85
   Grief's harmonics. 87
   Memorat memoria. 88
   July fugitive. 89
   To a snow-flake. 91
   Nocturn. 92
   A May burden. 93

A dead astronomer.	94
'Chose vue.'	95
'Whereto art thou come.'	96
Heaven and hell.	97
To a child.	98
Hermes.	99
House of bondage.	100
The heart.	101
A sunset.	102
Heard on the mountain.	104
ULTIMA.	107
Love's almsman plaineth his fare.	107
A holocaust.	108
Beneath a photograph.	109
After her going.	110
My lady the tyranness.	111
Unto this last.	113
Ultimum.	115
Envoy.	117

SIGHT AND INSIGHT

'Wisdom is easily seen by them that love her, and is found
by them that seek her.
To think therefore upon her is perfect understanding.'
WISDOM, vi.

THE MISTRESS OF VISION

I
>Secret was the garden;
>Set i' the pathless awe
>Where no star its breath can draw.
>Life, that is its warden,
>
>Sits behind the fosse of death. Mine eyes saw not, and I saw.

II
>It was a mazeful wonder;
>Thrice three times it was enwalled
>With an emerald—
>Seal-ed so asunder.
>
>All its birds in middle air hung a-dream, their music thralled.

III
>The Lady of fair weeping,
>At the garden's core,
>Sang a song of sweet and sore
>And the after-sleeping;
>
>In the land of Luthany, and the tracts of Elenore.

IV
>With sweet-panged singing,
>Sang she through a dream-night's day;
>That the bowers might stay,
>Birds bate their winging,
>
>Nor the wall of emerald float in wreath-ed haze away.

V
>The lily kept its gleaming,
>In her tears (divine conservers!)
>Wash-ed with sad art;
>And the flowers of dreaming
>Pal-ed not their fervours,
>For her blood flowed through their nervures;
>
>And the roses were most red, for she dipt them in her heart.

VI
    There was never moon,
    Save the white sufficing woman:
    Light most heavenly-human—
    Like the unseen form of sound,
    Sensed invisibly in tune,—
    With a sun-deriv-ed stole
    Did inaureole
    All her lovely body round;
Lovelily her lucid body with that light was interstrewn.

VII
    The sun which lit that garden wholly,
    Low and vibrant visible,
    Tempered glory woke;
    And it seem-ed solely
    Like a silver thurible
    Solemnly swung, slowly,
Fuming clouds of golden fire, for a cloud of incense smoke.

VIII
    But woe's me, and woe's me,
    For the secrets of her eyes!
    In my visions fearfully
    They are ever shown to be
    As fring-ed pools, whereof each lies
    Pallid-dark beneath the skies
    Of a night that is
    But one blear necropolis.
And her eyes a little tremble, in the wind of her own sighs.

IX
    Many changes rise on
    Their phantasmal mysteries.
    They grow to an horizon
    Where earth and heaven meet;
    And like a wing that dies on
    The vague twilight-verges,
    Many a sinking dream doth fleet
    Lessening down their secrecies.
    And, as dusk with day converges,
    Their orbs are troublously
Over-gloomed and over-glowed with hope and fear of things to be.

X
    There is a peak on Himalay,
    And on the peak undeluged snow,

And on the snow not eagles stray;
There if your strong feet could go,—
Looking over tow'rd Cathay
From the never-deluged snow—
Farthest ken might not survey
Where the peoples underground dwell whom antique fables know.

XI

East, ah, east of Himalay,
Dwell the nations underground;
Hiding from the shock of Day,
For the sun's uprising-sound:
Dare not issue from the ground
At the tumults of the Day,
So fearfully the sun doth sound
Clanging up beyond Cathay;
For the great earthquaking sunrise rolling up beyond Cathay.

XII

Lend me, O lend me
The terrors of that sound,
That its music may attend me.
Wrap my chant in thunders round;
While I tell the ancient secrets in that Lady's singing found.

XIII

On Ararat there grew a vine,
When Asia from her bathing rose;
Our first sailor made a twine
Thereof for his prefiguring brows.
Canst divine
Where, upon our dusty earth, of that vine a cluster grows?

XIV

On Golgotha there grew a thorn
Round the long-prefigured Brows.
Mourn, O mourn!
For the vine have we the spine? Is this all the Heaven allows?

XV

On Calvary was shook a spear;
Press the point into thy heart—
Joy and fear!
All the spines upon the thorn into curling tendrils start.

XVI
    O, dismay!
I, a wingless mortal, sporting
With the tresses of the sun?
I, that dare my hand to lay
On the thunder in its snorting?
    Ere begun,
Falls my singed song down the sky, even the old Icarian way.

XVII
    From the fall precipitant
These dim snatches of her chant
Only have remain-ed mine;—
That from spear and thorn alone
    May be grown
For the front of saint or singer any divinizing twine.

XVIII
    Her song said that no springing
Paradise but evermore
Hangeth on a singing
That has chords of weeping,
And that sings the after-sleeping
To souls which wake too sore.
'But woe the singer, woe!' she said; 'beyond the dead his singing-lore,
    All its art of sweet and sore,
He learns, in Elenore!'

XIX
    Where is the land of Luthany,
Where is the tract of Elenore?
I am bound therefor.

XX
    'Pierce thy heart to find the key;
With thee take
Only what none else would keep;
Learn to dream when thou dost wake,
Learn to wake when thou dost sleep.
Learn to water joy with tears,
Learn from fears to vanquish fears;
To hope, for thou dar'st not despair,
Exult, for that thou dar'st not grieve;
Plough thou the rock until it bear;
Know, for thou else couldst not believe;

Lose, that the lost thou may'st receive;
Die, for none other way canst live.
When earth and heaven lay down their veil,
And that apocalypse turns thee pale;
When thy seeing blindeth thee
To what thy fellow-mortals see;
When their sight to thee is sightless;
Their living, death; their light, most light-less;
Search no more—
Pass the gates of Luthany, tread the region Elenore.'

XXI

Where is the land of Luthany,
And where the region Elenore?
I do faint therefor.
'When to the new eyes of thee
All things by immortal power,
Near or far,
Hiddenly
To each other link-ed are,
That thou canst not stir a flower
Without troubling of a star;
When thy song is shield and mirror
To the fair snake-curl-ed Pain,
Where thou dar'st affront her terror
That on her thou may'st attain
Persean conquest; seek no more,
O seek no more!
Pass the gates of Luthany, tread the region Elenore.'

XXII

So sang she, so wept she,
Through a dream-night's day;
And with her magic singing kept she—
Mystical in music—
That garden of enchanting
In visionary May;
Swayless for my spirit's haunting,
Thrice-threefold walled with emerald from our mortal mornings grey.

XXIII

    And as a necromancer
    Raises from the rose-ash
    The ghost of the rose;
    My heart so made answer
    To her voice's silver plash,—
    Stirred in reddening flash,
And from out its mortal ruins the purpureal phantom blows.

XXIV

    Her tears made dulcet fretting,
    Her voice had no word,
    More than thunder or the bird.
    Yet, unforgetting,
The ravished soul her meanings knew. Mine ears heard not, and I heard.

XXV

    When she shall unwind
    All those wiles she wound about me,
    Tears shall break from out me,
    That I cannot find
Music in the holy poets to my wistful want, I doubt me!

CONTEMPLATION

This morning saw I, fled the shower,
The earth reclining in a lull of power:
The heavens, pursuing not their path,
Lay stretched out naked after bath,
Or so it seemed; field, water, tree, were still,
Nor was there any purpose on the calm-browed hill.

The hill, which sometimes visibly is
Wrought with unresting energies,
Looked idly; from the musing wood,
And every rock, a life renewed
Exhaled like an unconscious thought
When poets, dreaming unperplexed,
Dream that they dream of nought.
Nature one hour appears a thing unsexed,
Or to such serene balance brought
That her twin natures cease their sweet alarms,
And sleep in one another's arms.
The sun with resting pulses seems to brood,
And slacken its command upon my unurged blood.

The river has not any care
Its passionless water to the sea to bear;
The leaves have brown content;
The wall to me has freshness like a scent,
And takes half animate the air,
Making one life with its green moss and stain;
And life with all things seems too perfect blent
For anything of life to be aware.
The very shades on hill, and tree, and plain,
Where they have fallen doze, and where they doze remain.

No hill can idler be than I;
No stone its inter-particled vibration
Investeth with a stiller lie;
No heaven with a more urgent rest betrays
The eyes that on it gaze.
We are too near akin that thou shouldst cheat
Me, Nature, with thy fair deceit.

In poets floating like a water-flower
Upon the bosom of the glassy hour,
In skies that no man sees to move,

Lurk untumultuous vortices of power,
For joy too native, and for agitation
Too instant, too entire for sense thereof,
Motion like gnats when autumn suns are low,
Perpetual as the prisoned feet of love
On the heart's floors with pain-ed pace that go.
From stones and poets you may know,
Nothing so active is, as that which least seems so.

For he, that conduit running wine of song,
Then to himself does most belong,
When he his mortal house unbars
To the importunate and thronging feet
That round our corporal walls unheeded beat;
Till, all containing, he exalt
His stature to the stars, or stars
Narrow their heaven to his fleshly vault:
When, like a city under ocean,
To human things he grows a desolation,
And is made a habitation
For the fluctuous universe
To lave with unimpeded motion.
He scarcely frets the atmosphere
With breathing, and his body shares
The immobility of rocks;
His heart's a drop-well of tranquillity;
His mind more still is than the limbs of fear,
And yet its unperturbed velocity
The spirit of the simoom mocks.
He round the solemn centre of his soul
Wheels like a dervish, while his being is
Streamed with the set of the world's harmonies,
In the long draft of whatsoever sphere
He lists the sweet and clear
Clangour of his high orbit on to roll,
So gracious is his heavenly grace;
And the bold stars does hear,
Every one in his airy soar,
For evermore
Shout to each other from the peaks of space,
As thwart ravines of azure shouts the mountaineer.

'BY REASON OF THY LAW'

Here I make oath—
Although the heart that knows its bitterness
Hear loath,
And credit less—
That he who kens to meet Pain's kisses fierce
Which hiss against his tears,
Dread, loss, nor love frustrate,
Nor all iniquity of the froward years
Shall his inur-ed wing make idly bate,
Nor of the appointed quarry his staunch sight
To lose observance quite;
Seal from half-sad and all-elate
Sagacious eyes
Ultimate Paradise;
Nor shake his certitude of haughty fate.

Pacing the burning shares of many dooms,
I with stern tread do the clear-witting stars
To judgment cite,
If I have borne aright
The proving of their pure-willed ordeal.
From food of all delight
The heavenly Falconer my heart debars,
And tames with fearful glooms
The haggard to His call;
Yet sometimes comes a hand, sometimes a voice withal,
And she sits meek now, and expects the light.

In this Avernian sky,
This sultry and incumbent canopy
Of dull and doomed regret;
Where on the unseen verges yet, O yet,
At intervals,
Trembles, and falls,
Faint lightning of remembered transient sweet—
Ah, far too sweet
But to be sweet a little, a little sweet, and fleet;
Leaving this pallid trace,
This loitering and most fitful light a space,
Still some sad space,
For Grief to see her own poor face:-

Here where I keep my stand
With all o'er-anguished feet,
And no live comfort near on any hand;
Lo, I proclaim the unavoided term,
When this morass of tears, then drained and firm,
Shall be a land—
Unshaken I affirm—
Where seven-quired psalterings meet;
And all the gods move with calm hand in hand,
And eyes that know not trouble and the worm.

THE DREAD OF HEIGHT

IF ye were blind, ye should have no sin: but now ye say: We see: your sin remaineth. JOHN ix. 41.

    Not the Circean wine
    Most perilous is for pain:
    Grapes of the heavens' star-loaden vine,
    Whereto the lofty-placed
    Thoughts of fair souls attain,
    Tempt with a more retributive delight,
    And do disrelish all life's sober taste.
    'Tis to have drunk too well
    The drink that is divine,
    Maketh the kind earth waste,
    And breath intolerable.

    Ah me!
    How shall my mouth content it with mortality?
    Lo, secret music, sweetest music,
    From distances of distance drifting its lone flight,
    Down the arcane where Night would perish in night,
    Like a god's loosened locks slips undulously:
    Music that is too grievous of the height
    For safe and low delight,
    Too infinite,
    For bounded hearts which yet would girth the sea!

    So let it be,
    Though sweet be great, and though my heart be small:
    So let it be,
    O music, music, though you wake in me
    No joy, no joy at all;
    Although you only wake
    Uttermost sadness, measure of delight,
    Which else I could not credit to the height,
    Did I not know,
    That ill is statured to its opposite;
    Did I not know,
    And even of sadness so,
    Of utter sadness make,
    Of extreme sad a rod to mete
    The incredible excess of unsensed sweet,
    And mystic wall of strange felicity.
    So let it be,

Though sweet be great, and though my heart be small,
And bitter meat
The food of gods for men to eat;
Yea, John ate daintier, and did tread
Less ways of heat,
Than whom to their wind-carpeted
High banquet-hall,
And golden love-feasts, the fair stars entreat.

But ah withal,
Some hold, some stay,
O difficult Joy, I pray,
Some arms of thine,
Not only, only arms of mine!
Lest like a weary girl I fall
From clasping love so high,
And lacking thus thine arms, then may
Most hapless I
Turn utterly to love of basest rate;
For low they fall whose fall is from the sky.
Yea, who me shall secure
But I of height grown desperate
Surcease my wing, and my lost fate
Be dashed from pure
To broken writhings in the shameful slime:
Lower than man, for I dreamed higher,
Thrust down, by how much I aspire,
And damned with drink of immortality?
For such things be,
Yea, and the lowest reach of reeky Hell
Is but made possible
By forta'en breath of Heaven's austerest clime.

These tidings from the vast to bring
Needeth not doctor nor divine,
Too well, too well
My flesh doth know the heart-perturbing thing;
That dread theology alone
Is mine,
Most native and my own;
And ever with victorious toil
When I have made
Of the deific peaks dim escalade,
My soul with anguish and recoil
Doth like a city in an earthquake rock,

As at my feet the abyss is cloven then,
With deeper menace than for other men,
Of my potential cousinship with mire;
That all my conquered skies do grow a hollow mock,
My fearful powers retire,
No longer strong,
Reversing the shook banners of their song.

Ah, for a heart less native to high Heaven,
A hooded eye, for jesses and restraint,
Or for a will accipitrine to pursue!
The veil of tutelar flesh to simple livers given,
Or those brave-fledging fervours of the Saint,
Whose heavenly falcon-craft doth never taint,
Nor they in sickest time their ample virtue mew.

ORIENT ODE

Lo, in the sanctuaried East,
Day, a dedicated priest
In all his robes pontifical exprest,
Lifteth slowly, lifteth sweetly,
From out its Orient tabernacle drawn,
Yon orb-ed sacrament confest
Which sprinkles benediction through the dawn;
And when the grave procession's ceased,
The earth with due illustrious rite
Blessed,—ere the frail fingers featly
Of twilight, violet-cassocked acolyte,
His sacerdotal stoles unvest—
Sets, for high close of the mysterious feast,
The sun in august exposition meetly
Within the flaming monstrance of the West.
O salutaris hostia,
Quae coeli pandis ostium!
Through breach-ed darkness' rampart, a
Divine assaulter, art thou come!
God whom none may live and mark!
Borne within thy radiant ark,
While the Earth, a joyous David,
Dances before thee from the dawn to dark.
The moon, O leave, pale ruined Eve;
Behold her fair and greater daughter [2]
Offers to thee her fruitful water,
Which at thy first white Ave shall conceive!
Thy gazes do on simple her
Desirable allures confer;
What happy comelinesses rise
Beneath thy beautifying eyes!
Who was, indeed, at first a maid
Such as, with sighs, misgives she is not fair,
And secret views herself afraid,
Till flatteries sweet provoke the charms they swear:
Yea, thy gazes, blissful lover,
Make the beauties they discover!
What dainty guiles and treacheries caught
From artful prompting of love's artless thought
Her lowly loveliness teach her to adorn,
When thy plumes shiver against the conscious gates of morn!

---

[2] The earth.

And so the love which is thy dower,
Earth, though her first-frightened breast
Against the exigent boon protest,
(For she, poor maid, of her own power
Has nothing in herself, not even love,
But an unwitting void thereof),
Gives back to thee in sanctities of flower;
And holy odours do her bosom invest,
That sweeter grows for being prest:
Though dear recoil, the tremorous nurse of joy,
From thine embrace still startles coy,
Till Phosphor lead, at thy returning hour,
The laughing captive from the wishing West.

Nor the majestic heavens less
Thy formidable sweets approve,
Thy dreads and thy delights confess,
That do draw, and that remove.
Thou as a lion roar'st, O Sun,
Upon thy satellites' vex-ed heels;
Before thy terrible hunt thy planets run;
Each in his frighted orbit wheels,
Each flies through inassuageable chase,
Since the hunt o' the world begun,
The puissant approaches of thy face,
And yet thy radiant leash he feels.
Since the hunt o' the world begun,
Lashed with terror, leashed with longing,
The mighty course is ever run;
Pricked with terror, leashed with longing,
Thy rein they love, and thy rebuke they shun.
Since the hunt o' the world began,
With love that trembleth, fear that loveth,
Thou join'st the woman to the man;
And Life with Death
In obscure nuptials moveth,
Commingling alien, yet affin-ed breath.

Thou art the incarnated Light
Whose Sire is aboriginal, and beyond
Death and resurgence of our day and night;
From him is thy vicegerent wand
With double potence of the black and white.
Giver of Love, and Beauty, and Desire,
The terror, and the loveliness, and purging,

The deathfulness and lifefulness of fire!
Samson's riddling meanings merging
In thy twofold sceptre meet:
Out of thy minatory might,
Burning Lion, burning Lion,
Comes the honey of all sweet,
And out of thee, the eater, comes forth meat.
And though, by thine alternate breath,
Every kiss thou dost inspire
Echoeth
Back from the windy vaultages of death;
Yet thy clear warranty above
Augurs the wings of death too must
Occult reverberations stir of love
Crescent and life incredible;
That even the kisses of the just
Go down not unresurgent to the dust.
Yea, not a kiss which I have given,
But shall tri-umph upon my lips in heaven,
Or cling a shameful fungus there in hell.
Know'st thou me not, O Sun? Yea, well
Thou know'st the ancient miracle,
The children know'st of Zeus and May;
And still thou teachest them, O splendent Brother,
To incarnate, the antique way,
The truth which is their heritage from their Sire
In sweet disguise of flesh from their sweet Mother.
My fingers thou hast taught to con
Thy flame-chorded psalterion,
Till I can translate into mortal wire—
Till I can translate passing well—
The heavenly harping harmony,
Melodious, sealed, inaudible,
Which makes the dulcet psalter of the world's desire.
Thou whisperest in the Moon's white ear,
And she does whisper into mine,—
By night together, I and she—
With her virgin voice divine,
The things I cannot half so sweetly tell
As she can sweetly speak, I sweetly hear.

By her, the Woman, does Earth live, O Lord,
Yet she for Earth, and both in thee.
Light out of Light!
Resplendent and prevailing Word

Of the Unheard!
Not unto thee, great Image, not to thee
Did the wise heathen bend an idle knee;
And in an age of faith grown frore
If I too shall adore,
Be it accounted unto me
A bright sciential idolatry!
God has given thee visible thunders
To utter thine apocalypse of wonders;
And what want I of prophecy,
That at the sounding from thy station
Of thy flagrant trumpet, see
The seals that melt, the open revelation?
Or who a God-persuading angel needs,
That only heeds
The rhetoric of thy burning deeds?
Which but to sing, if it may be,
In worship-warranting moiety,
So I would win
In such a song as hath within
A smouldering core of mystery,
Brimm-ed with nimbler meanings up
Than hasty Gideons in their hands may sup;—
Lo, my suit pleads
That thou, Isaian coal of fire,
Touch from yon altar my poor mouth's desire,
And the relucent song take for thy sacred meeds.

To thine own shape
Thou round'st the chrysolite of the grape,
Bind'st thy gold lightnings in his veins;
Thou storest the white garners of the rains.
Destroyer and preserver, thou
Who medicinest sickness, and to health
Art the unthank-ed marrow of its wealth;
To those apparent sovereignties we bow
And bright appurtenances of thy brow!
Thy proper blood dost thou not give,
That Earth, the gusty Maenad, drink and dance?
Art thou not life of them that live?
Yea, in glad twinkling advent, thou dost dwell
Within our body as a tabernacle!
Thou bittest with thine ordinance
The jaws of Time, and thou dost mete
The unsustainable treading of his feet.

Thou to thy spousal universe
Art Husband, she thy Wife and Church;
Who in most dusk and vidual curch,
Her Lord being hence,
Keeps her cold sorrows by thy hearse.
The heavens renew their innocence
And morning state
But by thy sacrament communicate:
Their weeping night the symbol of our prayers,
Our darkened search,
And sinful vigil desolate.
Yea, biune in imploring dumb,
Essential Heavens and corporal Earth await,
The Spirit and the Bride say: Come!
Lo, of thy Magians I the least
Haste with my gold, my incenses and myrrhs,
To thy desired epiphany, from the spiced
Regions and odorous of Song's traded East.
Thou, for the life of all that live
The victim daily born and sacrificed;
To whom the pinion of this longing verse
Beats but with fire which first thyself did give,
To thee, O Sun—or is't perchance, to Christ?

Ay, if men say that on all high heaven's face
The saintly signs I trace
Which round my stol-ed altars hold their solemn place,
Amen, amen! For oh, how could it be,—
When I with wing-ed feet had run
Through all the windy earth about,
Quested its secret of the sun,
And heard what thing the stars together shout,—
I should not heed thereout
Consenting counsel won:-
'By this, O Singer, know we if thou see.
When men shall say to thee: Lo! Christ is here,
When men shall say to thee: Lo! Christ is there,
Believe them: yea, and this—then art thou seer,
When all thy crying clear
Is but: Lo here! lo there!—ah me, lo everywhere!'

NEW YEAR'S CHIMES

What is the song the stars sing?
  (And a million songs are as song of one.)
This is the song the stars sing:
  Sweeter song's none.

One to set, and many to sing,
  (And a million songs are as song of one),
One to stand, and many to cling,
The many things, and the one Thing,
  The one that runs not, the many that run.

The ever new weaveth the ever old
  (And a million songs are as song of one).
Ever telling the never told;
The silver saith, and the said is gold,
  And done ever the never done.

The chase that's chased is the Lord o' the chase
  (And a million songs are as song of one),
And the pursued cries on the race;
  And the hounds in leash are the hounds that run.

Hidden stars by the shown stars' sheen;
  (And a million suns are but as one);
Colours unseen by the colours seen,
And sounds unheard heard sounds between,
  And a night is in the light of the sun.

An ambuscade of light in night,
  (And a million secrets are but as one),
And a night is dark in the sun's light,
  And a world in the world man looks upon.

Hidden stars by the shown stars' wings,
  (And a million cycles are but as one),
And a world with unapparent strings
Knits the simulant world of things;
  Behold, and vision thereof is none.

The world above in the world below
  (And a million worlds are but as one),
And the One in all; as the sun's strength so
Strives in all strength, glows in all glow

Of the earth that wits not, and man thereon.

Braced in its own fourfold embrace
  (And a million strengths are as strength of one),
And round it all God's arms of grace,
The world, so as the Vision says,
  Doth with great lightning-tramples run.

And thunder bruiteth into thunder,
  (And a million sounds are as sound of one),
From stellate peak to peak is tossed a voice of wonder,
And the height stoops down to the depths thereunder,
  And sun leans forth to his brother-sun.

And the more ample years unfold
  (With a million songs as song of one),
A little new of the ever old,
A little told of the never told,
  Added act of the never done.

Loud the descant, and low the theme,
  (A million songs are as song of one);
And the dream of the world is dream in dream,
But the one Is is, or nought could seem;
  And the song runs round to the song begun.

This is the song the stars sing,
  (Ton-ed all in time);
Tintinnabulous, tuned to ring
A multitudinous-single thing,
  Rung all in rhyme.

FROM THE NIGHT OF FOREBEING.

AN ode after Easter.
 IN the chaos of preordination, and night of our forebeings.—
                                    SIR THOMAS BROWNE.
Et lux in tenebris erat, et tenebrae eam non comprehenderunt.—
                                    ST. JOHN.

>   Cast wide the folding doorways of the East,
>   For now is light increased!
>   And the wind-besomed chambers of the air,
>   See they be garnished fair;
>   And look the ways exhale some precious odours,
>   And set ye all about wild-breathing spice,
>   Most fit for Paradise.
>   Now is no time for sober gravity,
>   Season enough has Nature to be wise;
>   But now discinct, with raiment glittering free,
>   Shake she the ringing rafters of the skies
>   With festal footing and bold joyance sweet,
>   And let the earth be drunken and carouse!
>   For lo, into her house
>   Spring is come home with her world-wandering feet,
>   And all things are made young with young desires;
>   And all for her is light increased
>   In yellow stars and yellow daffodils,
>   And East to West, and West to East,
>   Fling answering welcome-fires,
>   By dawn and day-fall, on the jocund hills.
>   And ye, winged minstrels of her fair meinie,
>   Being newly coated in glad livery,
>   Upon her steps attend,
>   And round her treading dance and without end
>   Reel your shrill lutany.
>   What popular breath her coming does out-tell
>   The garrulous leaves among!
>   What little noises stir and pass
>   From blade to blade along the voluble grass!
>   O Nature, never-done
>   Ungaped-at Pentecostal miracle,
>   We hear thee, each man in his proper tongue!
>   Break, elemental children, break ye loose
>   From the strict frosty rule
>   Of grey-beard Winter's school.
>   Vault, O young winds, vault in your tricksome courses

Upon the snowy steeds that reinless use
In coerule pampas of the heaven to run;
Foaled of the white sea-horses,
Washed in the lambent waters of the sun.
Let even the slug-abed snail upon the thorn
Put forth a conscious horn!
Mine elemental co-mates, joy each one;
And ah, my foster-brethren, seem not sad—
No, seem not sad,
That my strange heart and I should be so little glad.
Suffer me at your leafy feast
To sit apart, a somewhat alien guest,
And watch your mirth,
Unsharing in the liberal laugh of earth;
Yet with a sympathy,
Begot of wholly sad and half-sweet memory—
The little sweetness making grief complete;
Faint wind of wings from hours that distant beat,
When I, I too,
Was once, O wild companions, as are you,
Ran with such wilful feet.
Wraith of a recent day and dead,
Risen wanly overhead,
Frail, strengthless as a noon-belated moon,
Or as the glazing eyes of watery heaven,
When the sick night sinks into deathly swoon.

A higher and a solemn voice
I heard through your gay-hearted noise;
A solemn meaning and a stiller voice
Sounds to me from far days when I too shall rejoice,
Nor more be with your jollity at strife.
O prophecy
Of things that are, and are not, and shall be!
The great-vanned Angel March
Hath trumpeted
His clangorous 'Sleep no more' to all the dead—
Beat his strong vans o'er earth, and air, and sea.
And they have heard;
Hark to the Jubilate of the bird
For them that found the dying way to life!
And they have heard,
And quicken to the great precursive word;
Green spray showers lightly down the cascade of the larch;
The graves are riven,

And the Sun comes with power amid the clouds of heaven!
Before his way
Went forth the trumpet of the March;
Before his way, before his way
Dances the pennon of the May!
O earth, unchilded, widowed Earth, so long
Lifting in patient pine and ivy-tree
Mournful belief and steadfast prophecy,
Behold how all things are made true!
Behold your bridegroom cometh in to you,
Exceeding glad and strong.
Raise up your eyes, O raise your eyes abroad!
No more shall you sit sole and vidual,
Searching, in servile pall,
Upon the hieratic night the star-sealed sense of all:
Rejoice, O barren, and look forth abroad!
Your children gathered back to your embrace
See with a mother's face.
Look up, O mortals, and the portent heed;
In very deed,
Washed with new fire to their irradiant birth,
Reintegrated are the heavens and earth!
From sky to sod,
The world's unfolded blossom smells of God.

O imagery
Of that which was the first, and is the last!
For as the dark, profound nativity,
God saw the end should be,
When the world's infant horoscope He cast.
Unshackled from the bright Phoebean awe,
In leaf, flower, mould, and tree,
Resolved into dividual liberty,
Most strengthless, unparticipant, inane,
Or suffered the ill peace of lethargy,
Lo, the Earth eased of rule:
Unsummered, granted to her own worst smart
The dear wish of the fool—
Disintegration, merely which man's heart
For freedom understands,
Amid the frog-like errors from the damp
And quaking swamp
Of the low popular levels spawned in all the lands.
But thou, O Earth, dost much disdain
The bondage of thy waste and futile reign,

And sweetly to the great compulsion draw
Of God's alone true-manumitting law,
And Freedom, only which the wise intend,
To work thine innate end.
Over thy vacant counterfeit of death
Broods with soft urgent breath
Love, that is child of Beauty and of Awe:
To intercleavage of sharp warring pain,
As of contending chaos come again,
Thou wak'st, O Earth,
And work'st from change to change and birth to birth
Creation old as hope, and new as sight;
For meed of toil not vain,
Hearing once more the primal fiat toll:-
'Let there be light!'
And there is light!
Light flagrant, manifest;
Light to the zenith, light from pole to pole;
Light from the East that waxeth to the West,
And with its puissant goings-forth
Encroaches on the South and on the North;
And with its great approaches does prevail
Upon the sullen fastness of the height,
And summoning its levied power
Crescent and confident through the crescent hour,
Goes down with laughters on the subject vale.
Light flagrant, manifest;
Light to the sentient closeness of the breast,
Light to the secret chambers of the brain!
And thou up-floatest, warm, and newly-bathed,
Earth, through delicious air,
And with thine own apparent beauties swathed,
Wringing the waters from thine arborous hair;
That all men's hearts, which do behold and see,
Grow weak with their exceeding much desire,
And turn to thee on fire,
Enamoured with their utter wish of thee,
Anadyomene!
What vine-outquickening life all creatures sup,
Feel, for the air within its sapphire cup
How it does leap, and twinkle headily!
Feel, for Earth's bosom pants, and heaves her scarfing sea;
And round and round in bacchanal rout reel the swift spheres
intemperably!

My little-worlded self! the shadows pass
In this thy sister-world, as in a glass,
Of all processions that revolve in thee:
Not only of cyclic Man
Thou here discern'st the plan,
Not only of cyclic Man, but of the cyclic Me.
Not solely of Mortality's great years
The reflex just appears,
But thine own bosom's year, still circling round
In ample and in ampler gyre
Toward the far completion, wherewith crowned,
Love unconsumed shall chant in his own furnace-fire.
How many trampled and deciduous joys
Enrich thy soul for joys deciduous still,
Before the distance shall fulfil
Cyclic unrest with solemn equipoise!
Happiness is the shadow of things past,
Which fools still take for that which is to be!
And not all foolishly:
For all the past, read true, is prophecy,
And all the firsts are hauntings of some Last,
And all the springs are flash-lights of one Spring.
Then leaf, and flower, and falless fruit
Shall hang together on the unyellowing bough;
And silence shall be Music mute
For her surcharg-ed heart. Hush thou!
These things are far too sure that thou should'st dream
Thereof, lest they appear as things that seem.

Shade within shade! for deeper in the glass
Now other imaged meanings pass;
And as the man, the poet there is read.
Winter with me, alack!
Winter on every hand I find:
Soul, brain, and pulses dead;
The mind no further by the warm sense fed,
The soul weak-stirring in the arid mind,
More tearless-weak to flash itself abroad
Than the earth's life beneath the frost-scorched sod.
My lips have drought, and crack,
By laving music long unvisited.
Beneath the austere and macerating rime
Draws back constricted in its icy urns
The genial flame of Earth, and there
With torment and with tension does prepare

The lush disclosures of the vernal time.
All joys draw inward to their icy urns,
Tormented by constraining rime,
And there
With undelight and throe prepare
The bounteous efflux of the vernal time.
Nor less beneath compulsive Law
Rebuk-ed draw
The numb-ed musics back upon my heart;
Whose yet-triumphant course I know
And prevalent pulses forth shall start,
Like cataracts that with thunderous hoof charge the disbanding snow.
All power is bound
In quickening refusal so;
And silence is the lair of sound;
In act its impulse to deliver,
With fluctuance and quiver
The endeavouring thew grows rigid;
Strong
From its retracted coil strikes the resilient song.

Giver of spring,
And song, and every young new thing!
Thou only seest in me, so stripped and bare,
The lyric secret waiting to be born,
The patient term allowed
Before it stretch and flutteringly unfold
Its rumpled webs of amethyst-freaked, diaphanous gold.
And what hard task abstracts me from delight,
Filling with hopeless hope and dear despair
The still-born day and parch-ed fields of night,
That my old way of song, no longer fair,
For lack of serene care,
Is grown a stony and a weed-choked plot,
Thou only know'st aright,
Thou only know'st, for I know not.
How many songs must die that this may live!
And shall this most rash hope and fugitive,
Fulfilled with beauty and with might
In days whose feet are rumorous on the air,
Make me forget to grieve
For songs which might have been, nor ever were?
Stern the denial, the travail slow,
The struggling wall will scantly grow:

And though with that dread rite of sacrifice
Ordained for during edifice,
How long, how long ago!
Into that wall which will not thrive
I build myself alive,
Ah, who shall tell me will the wall uprise?
Thou wilt not tell me, who dost only know!
Yet still in mind I keep,
He which observes the wind shall hardly sow,
He which regards the clouds shall hardly reap.
Thine ancient way! I give,
Nor wit if I receive;
Risk all, who all would gain: and blindly. Be it so.

'And blindly,' said I?—No!
That saying I unsay: the wings
Hear I not in praevenient winnowings
Of coming songs, that lift my hair and stir it?
What winds with music wet do the sweet storm foreshow!
Utter stagnation
Is the solstitial slumber of the spirit,
The blear and blank negation of all life:
But these sharp questionings mean strife, and strife
Is the negation of negation.
The thing from which I turn my troubled look
Fearing the gods' rebuke;
That perturbation putting glory on,
As is the golden vortex in the West
Over the foundered sun;
That—but low breathe it, lest the Nemesis
Unchild me, vaunting this—
Is bliss, the hid, hugged, swaddled bliss!
O youngling Joy carest!
That on my now first-mothered breast
Pliest the strange wonder of thine infant lip,
What this aghast surprise of keenest panging,
Wherefrom I blench, and cry thy soft mouth rest?
Ah hold, withhold, and let the sweet mouth slip!
So, with such pain, recoils the woolly dam,
Unused, affrighted, from her yeanling lamb:
I, one with her in cruel fellowship,
Marvel what unmaternal thing I am.

Nature, enough! within thy glass
Too many and too stern the shadows pass.
In this delighted season, flaming
For thy resurrection-feast,
Ah, more I think the long ensepulture cold,
Than stony winter rolled
From the unsealed mouth of the holy East;
The snowdrop's saintly stoles less heed
Than the snow-cloistered penance of the seed.
'Tis the weak flesh reclaiming
Against the ordinance
Which yet for just the accepting spirit scans.
Earth waits, and patient heaven,
Self-bonded God doth wait
Thrice-promulgated bans
Of his fair nuptial-date.
And power is man's,
With that great word of 'wait,'
To still the sea of tears,
And shake the iron heart of Fate.
In that one word is strong
An else, alas, much-mortal song;
With sight to pass the frontier of all spheres,
And voice which does my sight such wrong.

Not without fortitude I wait
The dark majestical ensuit
Of destiny, nor peevish rate
Calm-knowledged Fate.
I, that no part have in the time's bragged way,
And its loud bruit
I, in this house so rifted, marred,
So ill to live in, hard to leave;
I, so star-weary, over-warred,
That have no joy in this your day—
Rather foul fume englutting, that of day
Confounds all ray—
But only stand aside and grieve;
I yet have sight beyond the smoke,
And kiss the gods' feet, though they wreak
Upon me stroke and again stroke;
And this my seeing is not weak.
The Woman I behold, whose vision seek
All eyes and know not; t'ward whom climb
The steps o' the world, and beats all wing of rhyme,

And knows not; 'twixt the sun and moon
Her inexpressible front enstarred
Tempers the wrangling spheres to tune;
Their divergent harmonies
Concluded in the concord of her eyes,
And vestal dances of her glad regard.
I see, which fretteth with surmise
Much heads grown unsagacious-grey,
The slow aim of wise-hearted Time,
Which folded cycles within cycles cloak:
We pass, we pass, we pass; this does not pass away,
But holds the furrowing earth still harnessed to its yoke.
The stars still write their golden purposes
On heaven's high palimpsest, and no man sees,
Nor any therein Daniel; I do hear
From the revolving year
A voice which cries:
'All dies;
Lo, how all dies! O seer,
And all things too arise:
All dies, and all is born;
But each resurgent morn, behold, more near the Perfect Morn.'

Firm is the man, and set beyond the cast
Of Fortune's game, and the iniquitous hour,
Whose falcon soul sits fast,
And not intends her high sagacious tour
Or ere the quarry sighted; who looks past
To slow much sweet from little instant sour,
And in the first does always see the last.

ANY SAINT

His shoulder did I hold
Too high that I, o'erbold
    Weak one,
      Should lean thereon.

But He a little hath
Declined His stately path
    And my
      Feet set more high;

That the slack arm may reach
His shoulder, and faint speech
    Stir
      His unwithering hair.

And bolder now and bolder
I lean upon that shoulder
    So dear
      He is and near:

And with His aureole
The tresses of my soul
    Are blent
      In wished content.

Yes, this too gentle Lover
Hath flattering words to move her
    To pride
      By His sweet side.

Ah, Love! somewhat let be!
Lest my humility
    Grow weak
      When thou dost speak!

Rebate thy tender suit,
Lest to herself impute
    Some worth
      Thy bride of earth!

A maid too easily
Conceits herself to be
    Those things

Her lover sings;

And being straitly wooed,
Believes herself the Good
    And Fair
  He seeks in her.

Turn something of Thy look,
And fear me with rebuke,
    That I
  May timorously

Take tremors in Thy arms,
And with contriv-ed charms
    Allure
  A love unsure.

Not to me, not to me,
Builded so flawfully,
    O God,
  Thy humbling laud!

Not to this man, but Man,—
Universe in a span;
    Point
  Of the spheres conjoint;

In whom eternally
Thou, Light, dost focus Thee!—
    Didst pave
  The way o' the wave;

Rivet with stars the Heaven,
For causeways to Thy driven
    Car
  In its coming far

Unto him, only him;
In Thy deific whim
    Didst bound
  Thy works' great round

In this small ring of flesh;
The sky's gold-knotted mesh
    Thy wrist
    Did only twist

To take him in that net.—
Man! swinging-wicket set
    Between
    The Unseen and Seen;

Lo, God's two worlds immense,
Of spirit and of sense,
    Wed
    In this narrow bed;

Yea, and the midge's hymn
Answers the seraphim
    Athwart
    Thy body's court!

Great arm-fellow of God!
To the ancestral clod
    Kin,
    And to cherubin;

Bread predilectedly
O' the worm and Deity!
    Hark,
    O God's clay-sealed Ark,

To praise that fits thee, clear
To the ear within the ear,
    But dense
    To clay-sealed sense.

All the Omnific made
When in a word he said,
    (Mystery!)
    He uttered THEE;

Thee His great utterance bore,
O secret metaphor
    Of what
    Thou dream'st no jot!

Cosmic metonymy!
Weak world-unshuttering key!
    One
  Seal of Solomon!

Trope that itself not scans
Its huge significance,
    Which tries
  Cherubic eyes.

Primer where the angels all
God's grammar spell in small,
    Nor spell
  The highest too well.

Point for the great descants
Of starry disputants;
    Equation
  Of creation.

Thou meaning, couldst thou see,
Of all which dafteth thee;
    So plain,
  It mocks thy pain;

Stone of the Law indeed,
Thine own self couldst thou read;
    Thy bliss
  Within thee is.

Compost of Heaven and mire,
Slow foot and swift desire!
    Lo,
  To have Yes, choose No;

Gird, and thou shalt unbind;
Seek not, and thou shalt find;
    To eat,
  Deny thy meat;

And thou shalt be fulfilled
With all sweet things unwilled:
    So best
  God loves to jest

With children small—a freak
Of heavenly hide-and-seek
   Fit
  For thy wayward wit,

Who art thyself a thing
Of whim and wavering;
   Free
  When His wings pen thee;

Sole fully blest, to feel
God whistle thee at heel;
   Drunk up
  As a dew-drop,

When He bends down, sun-wise,
Intemperable eyes;
   Most proud,
  When utterly bowed.

To feel thyself and be
His dear nonentity—
   Caught
  Beyond human thought

In the thunder-spout of Him,
Until thy being dim,
   And be
  Dead deathlessly.

Stoop, stoop; for thou dost fear
The nettle's wrathful spear,
   So slight
  Art thou of might!

Rise; for Heaven hath no frown
When thou to thee pluck'st down,
   Strong clod!
  The neck of God.

ASSUMPTA MARIA

'THOU needst not sing new songs, but say the old.'—COWLEY.

    Mortals, that behold a Woman,
      Rising 'twixt the Moon and Sun;
    Who am I the heavens assume? an
      All am I, and I am one.

    Multitudinous ascend I,
      Dreadful as a battle arrayed,
    For I bear you whither tend I;
      Ye are I: be undismayed!
    I, the Ark that for the graven
      Tables of the Law was made;
    Man's own heart was one, one Heaven,
      Both within my womb were laid.
      For there Anteros with Eros
        Heaven with man conjoin-ed was,—
      Twin-stone of the Law, Ischyros,
        Agios Athanatos.

    I, the flesh-girt Paradises
      Gardenered by the Adam new,
    Daintied o'er with sweet devices
      Which He loveth, for He grew.
    I, the boundless strict savannah
      Which God's leaping feet go through;
    I, the heaven whence the Manna,
      Weary Israel, slid on you!
      He the Anteros and Eros,
        I the body, He the Cross;
      He upbeareth me, Ischyros,
        Agios Athanatos!

I am Daniel's mystic Mountain,
  Whence the mighty stone was rolled;
I am the four Rivers' fountain,
  Watering Paradise of old;
Cloud down-raining the Just One am,
  Danae of the Shower of Gold;
I the Hostel of the Sun am;
  He the Lamb, and I the Fold.
    He the Anteros and Eros,
      I the body, He the Cross;
    He is fast to me, Ischyros,
      Agios Athanatos!

I, the presence-hall where Angels
  Do enwheel their plac-ed King—
Even my thoughts which, without change else,
  Cyclic burn and cyclic sing.
To the hollow of Heaven transplanted,
  I a breathing Eden spring,
Where with venom all outpanted
  Lies the slimed Curse shrivelling.
    For the brazen Serpent clear on
      That old fang-ed knowledge shone;
    I to Wisdom rise, Ischyron,
      Agion Athanaton!

See in highest heaven pavilioned
  Now the maiden Heaven rest,
The many-breasted sky out-millioned
  By the splendours of her vest.
Lo, the Ark this holy tide is
  The un-handmade Temple's guest,
And the dark Egyptian bride is
  Whitely to the Spouse-Heart prest!
    He the Anteros and Eros,
      Nail me to Thee, sweetest Cross!
    He is fast to me, Ischyros,
      Agios Athanatos!

'Tell me, tell me, O Belov-ed,
  Where Thou dost in mid-day feed!
For my wanderings are reprov-ed,
  And my heart is salt with need.'
'Thine own self not spellest God in,
  Nor the lisping papyrus reed?

Follow where the flocks have trodden,
  Follow where the shepherds lead.'
    He, the Anteros and Eros,
      Mounts me in AEgyptic car,
    Twin-yoked; leading me, Ischyros,
      Trembling to the untempted Far.

'Make me chainlets, silvern, golden,
  I that sow shall surely reap;
While as yet my Spouse is holden
  Like a Lion in mountained sleep.'
'Make her chainlets, silvern, golden,
  She hath sown and she shall reap;
Look up to the mountains olden,
  Whence help comes with lioned leap.'
    By what gushed the bitter Spear on,
      Pain, which sundered, maketh one;
    Crucified to Him, Ischyron,
      Agion Athanaton!

Then commanded and spake to me
  He who framed all things that be;
And my Maker entered through me,
  In my tent His rest took He.
Lo! He standeth, Spouse and Brother;
  I to Him, and He to me,
Who upraised me where my mother
  Fell, beneath the apple-tree.
    Risen 'twixt Anteros and Eros,
      Blood and Water, Moon and Sun,
    He upbears me, He Ischyros,
      I bear Him, the Athanaton!

Where is laid the Lord arisen?
  In the light we walk in gloom;
Though the sun has burst his prison,
  We know not his biding-room.
Tell us where the Lord sojourneth,
  For we find an empty tomb.
'Whence He sprung, there He returneth,
  Mystic Sun,—the Virgin's Womb.'
    Hidden Sun, His beams so near us,
      Cloud enpillared as He was
    From of old, there He, Ischyros,
      Waits our search, Athanatos.

Who will give Him me for brother,
  Counted of my family,
Sucking the sweet breasts of my Mother?—
  I His flesh, and mine is He;
To my Bread myself the bread is,
  And my Wine doth drink me: see,
His left hand beneath my head is,
  His right hand embraceth me!
    Sweetest Anteros and Eros,
      Lo, her arms He leans across;
    Dead that we die not, stooped to rear us,
      Thanatos Athanatos.

Who is She, in candid vesture,
  Rushing up from out the brine?
Treading with resilient gesture
  Air, and with that Cup divine?
She in us and we in her are,
  Beating Godward: all that pine,
Lo, a wonder and a terror!
  The Sun hath blushed the Sea to Wine!
    He the Anteros and Eros,
      She the Bride and Spirit; for
    Now the days of promise near us,
      And the Sea shall be no more.

Open wide thy gates, O Virgin,
  That the King may enter thee!
At all gates the clangours gurge in,
  God's paludament lightens, see!
Camp of Angels! Well we even
  Of this thing may doubtful be,—
If thou art assumed to Heaven,
  Or is Heaven assumed to thee!
    Consummatum. Christ the promised,
      Thy maiden realm is won, O Strong!
    Since to such sweet Kingdom comest,
      Remember me, poor Thief of Song!

Cadent fails the stars along:-
  Mortals, that behold a woman
    Rising 'twixt the Moon and Sun;
Who am I the heavens assume? an
  All am I, and I am one.

THE AFTER WOMAN

Daughter of the ancient Eve,
We know the gifts ye gave—and give.
Who knows the gifts which YOU shall give,
Daughter of the newer Eve?
You, if my soul be augur, you
Shall—O what shall you not, Sweet, do?
The celestial traitress play,
And all mankind to bliss betray;
With sacrosanct cajoleries
And starry treachery of your eyes,
Tempt us back to Paradise!
Make heavenly trespass;—ay, press in
Where faint the fledge-foot seraphin,
Blest Fool! Be ensign of our wars,
And shame us all to warriors!
Unbanner your bright locks,—advance
Girl, their gilded puissance,
I' the mystic vaward, and draw on
After the lovely gonfalon
Us to out-folly the excess
Of your sweet foolhardiness;
To adventure like intense
Assault against Omnipotence!

Give me song, as She is, new,
Earth should turn in time thereto!
New, and new, and thrice so new,
All old sweets, New Sweet, meant you!
Fair, I had a dream of thee,
When my young heart beat prophecy,
And in apparition elate
Thy little breasts knew wax-ed great,
Sister of the Canticle,
And thee for God grown marriageable.
How my desire desired your day,
That, wheeled in rumour on its way,
Shook me thus with presentience! Then
Eden's lopped tree shall shoot again:
For who Christ's eyes shall miss, with those
Eyes for evident nuncios?
Or who be tardy to His call
In your accents augural?

Who shall not feel the Heavens hid
Impend, at tremble of your lid,
And divine advent shine avowed
Under that dim and lucid cloud;
Yea, 'fore the silver apocalypse
Fail, at the unsealing of your lips?
When to love YOU is (O Christ's Spouse!)
To love the beauty of His house;
Then come the Isaian days; the old
Shall dream; and our young men behold
Vision—yea, the vision of Thabor mount,
Which none to other shall recount,
Because in all men's hearts shall be
The seeing and the prophecy.
For ended is the Mystery Play,
When Christ is life, and you the way;
When Egypt's spoils are Israel's right,
And Day fulfils the married arms of Night.
But here my lips are still.
Until
You and the hour shall be revealed,
This song is sung and sung not, and its words are sealed.

GRACE OF THE WAY

'My brother!' spake she to the sun;
  The kindred kisses of the stars
Were hers; her feet were set upon
  The moon. If slumber solved the bars

Of sense, or sense transpicuous grown
  Fulfill-ed seeing unto sight,
I know not; nor if 'twas my own
  Ingathered self that made her night.

The windy trammel of her dress,
  Her blown locks, took my soul in mesh;
God's breath they spake, with visibleness
  That stirred the raiment of her flesh:

And sensible, as her blown were,
  Beyond the precincts of her form
I felt the woman flow from her—
  A calm of intempestuous storm.

I failed against the affluent tide;
  Out of this abject earth of me
I was translated and enskied
  Into the heavenly-regioned She.

Now of that vision I bereaven
  This knowledge keep, that may not dim:-
Short arm needs man to reach to Heaven,
  So ready is Heaven to stoop to him.

Which sets, to measure of man's feet,
  No alien Tree for trysting-place;
And who can read, may read the sweet
  Direction in his Lady's face.

And pass and pass the daily crowd,
  Unwares, occulted Paradise;
Love the lost plot cries silver-loud,
  Nor any know the tongue he cries.

The light is in the darkness, and
  The darkness doth not comprehend:
God hath no haste; and God's sons stand
  Yet a Day, tarrying for the end.

Dishonoured Rahab still hath hid,
  Yea still, within her house of shame,
The messengers by Jesus bid
  Forerun the coming of His Name.

The Word was flesh, and crucified,
  From the beginning, and blasphemed:
Its profaned raiment men divide,
  Damned by what, reverenced, had redeemed.

Thy Lady, was thy heart not blind,
  One hour gave to thy witless trust
The key thou go'st about to find;
  And thou hast dropped it in the dust.

Of her, the Way's one mortal grace,
  Own, save thy seeing be all forgot,
That truly, God was in this place,
  And thou, unbless-ed, knew'st it not.

But some have eyes, and will not see;
  And some would see, and have not eyes;
And fail the tryst, yet find the Tree,
  And take the lesson for the prize.

RETROSPECT

Alas, and I have sung
Much song of matters vain,
And a heaven-sweetened tongue
Turned to unprofiting strain
Of vacant things, which though
Even so they be, and throughly so,
It is no boot at all for thee to know,
But babble and false pain.

What profit if the sun
Put forth his radiant thews,
And on his circuit run,
Even after my device, to this and to that use;
And the true Orient, Christ,
Make not His cloud of thee?
I have sung vanity,
And nothing well devised.

And though the cry of stars
Give tongue before his way
Goldenly as I say,
And each from wide Saturnus to hot Mars
He calleth by its name,
Lest that its bright feet stray;
And thou have lore of all,
But to thine own Sun's call
Thy path disorbed hast never wit to tame;
It profits not withal,
And my rede is but lame.

Only that, 'mid vain vaunt
Of wisdom ignorant,
A little kiss upon the feet of Love
My hasty verse has stayed
Sometimes a space to plant:
It has not wholly strayed,
Not wholly missed near sweet, fanning proud plumes above.

Therefore I do repent
That with religion vain,
And misconceiv-ed pain,
I have my music bent
To waste on bootless things its skiey-gendered rain:
Yet shall a wiser day
Fulfil more heavenly way,
And with approv-ed music clear this slip
I trust in God most sweet;
Meantime the silent lip,
Meantime the climbing feet.

A NARROW VESSEL

BEING a little dramatic sequence on the aspect of primitive girl-nature towards a love beyond its capacities.

A GIRL'S SIN

I.—In her eyes.
    Cross child! red, and frowning so?
      'I, the day just over,
    Gave a lock of hair to—no!
      How DARE you say, my lover?'

    He asked you?—Let me understand;
      Come, child, let me sound it!
    'Of course, he WOULD have asked it, and—
      And so—somehow—he—found it.

    'He told it out with great loud eyes—
      Men have such little wit!
    His sin I ever will chastise
      Because I gave him it.

    'Shameless in me the gift, alas!
      In him his open bliss:
    But for the privilege he has
      A thousand he shall miss!

    'His eyes, where once I dreadless laughed,
      Call up a burning blot:
    I hate him, for his shameful craft
      That asked by asking not!'

    Luckless boy! and all for hair
      He never asked, you said?
    'Not just—but then he gazed—I swear
      He gazed it from my head!

    'His silence on my cheek like breath
      I felt in subtle way;
    More sweet than aught another saith
      Was what he did not say.

    'He'll think me vanquished, for this lapse,

Who should be above him;
Perhaps he'll think me light; perhaps—
   Perhaps he'll think I—love him!

'Are his eyes conscious and elate,
   I hate him that I blush;
Or are they innocent, still I hate—
   They mean a thing's to hush.

'Before he nought amiss could do,
   Now all things show amiss;
'Twas all my fault, I know that true,
   But all my fault was his.

'I hate him for his mute distress,
   'Tis insult he should care!
Because my heart's all humbleness,
   All pride is in my air.

'With him, each favour that I do
   Is bold suit's hallowing text;
Each gift a bastion levelled, to
   The next one and the next.

'Each wish whose grant may him befall
   Is clogged by those withstood;
He trembles, hoping one means all,
   And I, lest perhaps it should.

'Behind me piecemeal gifts I cast,
   My fleeing self to save;
And that's the thing must go at last,
   For that's the thing he'd have.

'My lock the enforc-ed steel did grate
   To cut; its root-thrills came
Down to my bosom. It might sate
   His lust for my poor shame!

'His sifted dainty this should be
   For a score ambrosial years!
But his too much humility
   Alarums me with fears.

'My gracious grace a breach he counts
  For graceless escalade;
And, though he's silent ere he mounts,
  My watch is not betrayed.

'My heart hides from my soul he's sweet:
  Ah dread, if he divine!
One touch, I might fall at his feet,
  And he might rise from mine.

'To hear him praise my eyes' brown gleams
  Was native, safe delight;
But now it usurpation seems,
  Because I've given him right.

'Before I'd have him not remove,
  Now would not have him near;
With sacrifice I called on Love,
  And the apparition's Fear.'

Foolish to give it!—'Twas my whim,
  When he might parted be,
To think that I should stay by him
  In a little piece of me.

'He always said my hair was soft—
  What touches he will steal!
Each touch and look (and he'll look oft)
  I almost thought I'd feel.

'And then, when first he saw the hair,
  To think his dear amazement!
As if he wished from skies a star,
  And found it in his casement.

'He's kiss the lock—and I had toyed
  With dreamed delight of this:
But ah, in proof, delight was void—
  I could not SEE his kiss!'

So, fond one, half this agony
  Were spared, which my hand hushes,
Could you have played, Sweet, the sweet spy,
  And blushed not for your blushes!

A GIRL'S SIN

II.—In his eyes.

    Can I forget her cruelty
    Who, brown miracle, gave you me?
    Or with unmoisted eyes think on
    The proud surrender overgone,
    (Lowlihead in haughty dress),
    Of the tender tyranness?
    And ere thou for my joy was given,
    How rough the road to that blest heaven!
    With what pangs I fore-expiated
    Thy cold outlawry from her head;
    How was I trampled and brought low,
    Because her virgin neck was so;
    How thralled beneath the jealous state
    She stood at point to abdicate;
    How sacrificed, before to me
    She sacrificed her pride and thee;
    How did she, struggling to abase
    Herself to do me strange, sweet grace,
    Enforce unwitting me to share
    Her throes and abjectness with her;
    Thence heightening that hour when her lover
    Her grace, with trembling, should discover,
    And in adoring trouble be
    Humbled at her humility!
    And with what pitilessness was I
    After slain, to pacify
    The uneasy manes of her shame,
    Her haunting blushes!—Mine the blame:
    What fair injustice did I rue
    For what I—did not tempt her to?
    Nor aught the judging maid might win
    Me to assoil from HER sweet sin.
    But nought were extreme punishment
    For that beyond-divine content,
    When my with-thee-first-giddied eyes
    Stooped ere their due on Paradise!
    O hour of consternating bliss
    When I heavened me in thy kiss;
    Thy softness (daring overmuch!)
    Profan-ed with my licensed touch;
    Worshipped, with tears, on happy knee,
    Her doubt, her trust, her shyness free,
    Her timorous audacity!

LOVE DECLARED

I looked, she drooped, and neither spake, and cold,
We stood, how unlike all forecasted thought
Of that desir-ed minute! Then I leaned
Doubting; whereat she lifted—oh, brave eyes
Unfrighted:—forward like a wind-blown flame
Came bosom and mouth to mine!
     That falling kiss
Touching long-laid expectance, all went up
Suddenly into passion; yea, the night
Caught, blazed, and wrapt us round in vibrant fire.

  Time's beating wing subsided, and the winds
Caught up their breathing, and the world's great pulse
Stayed in mid-throb, and the wild train of life
Reeled by, and left us stranded on a hush.
This moment is a statue unto Love
Carved from a fair white silence.
     Lo, he stands
Within us—are we not one now, one, one roof,
His roof, and the partition of weak flesh
Gone down before him, and no more, for ever?—
Stands like a bird new-lit, and as he lit,
Poised in our quiet being; only, only
Within our shaken hearts the air of passion,
Cleft by his sudden coming, eddies still
And whirs round his enchanted movelessness.

A film of trance between two stirrings! Lo,
It bursts; yet dream's snapped links cling round the limbs
Of waking: like a running evening stream
Which no man hears, or sees, or knows to run,
(Glazed with dim quiet), save that there the moon
Is shattered to a creamy flicker of flame,
Our eyes' sweet trouble were hid, save that the love
Trembles a little on their impassioned calms.

THE WAY OF A MAID

The lover whose soul shaken is
In some decuman billow of bliss,
Who feels his gradual-wading feet
Sink in some sudden hollow of sweet,
And 'mid love's us-ed converse comes
Sharp on a mood which all joy sums—
An instant's fine compendium of
The liberal-leav-ed writ of love;
His abashed pulses beating thick
At the exigent joy and quick,
Is dumbed, by aiming utterance great
Up to the miracle of his fate.
The wise girl, such Icarian fall
Saved by her confidence that she's small,—
As what no kindred word will fit
Is uttered best by opposite,
Love in the tongue of hate exprest,
And deepest anguish in a jest,—
Feeling the infinite must be
Best said by triviality,
Speaks, where expression bates its wings,
Just happy, alien, little things;
What of all words is in excess
Implies in a sweet nothingness,
With dailiest babble shows her sense
That full speech were full impotence;
And while she feels the heavens lie bare,
She only talks about her hair.

BEGINNING OF END

She was aweary of the hovering
Of Love's incessant tumultuous wing;
Her lover's tokens she would answer not—
'Twere well she should be strange with him somewhat:
A pretty babe, this Love,—but fie on it,
That would not suffer her lay it down a whit!
Appointed tryst defiantly she balked,
And with her lightest comrade lightly walked,
Who scared the chidden Love to hide apart,
And peep from some unnoticed corner of her heart.
She thought not of her lover, deem it not
(There yonder, in the hollow, that's HIS cot),
But she forgot not that he was forgot.
She saw him at his gate, yet stilled her tongue—
So weak she felt her, that she would feel strong,
And she must punish him for doing him wrong:
Passed, unoblivious of oblivion still;
And if she turned upon the brow o' the hill,
It was so openly, so lightly done,
You saw she thought he was not thought upon.
He through the gate went back in bitterness;
She that night woke and stirred, with no distress,
Glad of her doing,—sedulous to be glad,
Lest perhaps her foolish heart suspect that it was sad.

PENELOPE

Love, like a wind, shook wide your blosmy eyes,
You trembled, and your breath came sobbing-wise
  For that you loved me.

You were so kind, so sweet, none could withhold
To adore, but that you were so strange, so cold;
  For that you loved me.

Like to a box of spikenard did you break
Your heart about my feet. What words you spake!
  For that you loved me.

Life fell to dust without me; so you tried
All carefullest ways to drive me from your side,
  For that you loved me.

You gave yourself as children give, that weep
And snatch back, with—'I meant you not to keep!'
  For that you loved me.

I am no woman, girl, nor ever knew
That love could teach all ways that hate could do
  To her that loved me.

Have less of love, or less of woman in
Your love, or loss may even from this begin—
  That you so love me.

For, wild Penelope, the web you wove
You still unweave, unloving all your love;
  Is this to love me,

Or what rights have I that scorn could deny?
Even of your love, alas, poor Love must die,
  If so you love me!

THE END OF IT

She did not love to love; but hated him
For making her to love, and so her whim
From passion taught misprision to begin;
And all this sin
Was because love to cast out had no skill
Self, which was regent still.
Her own self-will made void her own self's will

EPILOGUE

If I have studied here in part
A tale as old as maiden's heart,
   'Tis that I do see herein
   Shadow of more piteous sin.

She, that but giving part, not whole,
Took even the part back, is the Soul:
   And that so disdain-ed Lover—
   Best unthought, since Love is over.

Love to invite, desire, and fear,
And Love's exactions cost too dear
   Count for Love's possession,—ah,
   Thy way, misera Anima!

To give the pledge, and yet be pined
That a pledge should have force to bind,
   This, O Soul, too often still
   Is the recreance of thy will!

Out of Love's arms to make fond chain,
And, because struggle bringeth pain,
   Hate Love for Love's sweet constraint,
   Is the way of Souls that faint.

Such a Soul, for saddest end,
Finds Love the foe in Love the friend;
   And—ah, grief incredible!—
   Treads the way of Heaven, to Hell.

MISCELLANEOUS ODES

ODE TO THE SETTING SUN

PRELUDE.
>The wailful sweetness of the violin
>>Floats down the hush-ed waters of the wind,
>The heart-strings of the throbbing harp begin
>>To long in aching music. Spirit-pined,

>In wafts that poignant sweetness drifts, until
>>The wounded soul ooze sadness. The red sun,
>A bubble of fire, drops slowly toward the hill,
>>While one bird prattles that the day is done.

>O setting Sun, that as in reverent days
>>Sinkest in music to thy smooth-ed sleep,
>Discrowned of homage, though yet crowned with rays,
>>Hymned not at harvest more, though reapers reap:

>For thee this music wakes not. O deceived,
>>If thou hear in these thoughtless harmonies
>A pious phantom of adorings reaved,
>>And echo of fair ancient flatteries!

>Yet, in this field where the Cross planted reigns,
>>I know not what strange passion bows my head
>To thee, whose great command upon my veins
>>Proves thee a god for me not dead, not dead!

>For worship it is too incredulous,
>>For doubt—oh, too believing-passionate!
>What wild divinity makes my heart thus
>>A fount of most baptismal tears?—Thy straight

>Long beam lies steady on the Cross. Ah me!
>>What secret would thy radiant finger show?
>Of thy bright mastership is this the key?
>>Is THIS thy secret, then? And is it woe?

>Fling from thine ear the burning curls, and hark
>>A song thou hast not heard in Northern day;
>For Rome too daring, and for Greece too dark,
>>Sweet with wild wings that pass, that pass away!

ODE

Alpha and Omega, sadness and mirth,
  The springing music, and its wasting breath—
The fairest things in life are Death and Birth,
  And of these two the fairer thing is Death.
Mystical twins of Time inseparable,
  The younger hath the holier array,
    And hath the awfuller sway:
  It is the falling star that trails the light,
  It is the breaking wave that hath the might,
The passing shower that rainbows maniple.
  Is it not so, O thou down-stricken Day,
That draw'st thy splendours round thee in thy fall?
High was thine Eastern pomp inaugural;
But thou dost set in statelier pageantry,
  Lauded with tumults of a firmament:
Thy visible music-blasts make deaf the sky,
  Thy cymbals clang to fire the Occident,
Thou dost thy dying so triumphally:
I SEE the crimson blaring of thy shawms!
    Why do those lucent palms
Strew thy feet's failing thicklier than their might,
Who dost but hood thy glorious eyes with night,
And vex the heels of all the yesterdays?
    Lo! this loud, lackeying praise
Will stay behind to greet the usurping moon,
  When they have cloud-barred over thee the West.
Oh, shake the bright dust from thy parting shoon!
  The earth not paeans thee, nor serves thy hest,
Be godded not by Heaven! avert thy face,
    And leave to blank disgrace
The oblivious world! unsceptre thee of state and place!

Ha! but bethink thee what thou gazedst on,
  Ere yet the snake Decay had venomed tooth;
The name thou bar'st in those vast seasons gone—
    Candid Hyperion,
  Clad in the light of thine immortal youth!
  Ere Dionysus bled thy vines,
Or Artemis drave her clamours through the wood,
    Thou saw'st how once against Olympus' height
      The brawny Titans stood,
And shook the gods' world 'bout their ears, and how
Enceladus (whom Etna cumbers now)

Shouldered me Pelion with its swinging pines,
The river unrecked, that did its broken flood
Spurt on his back: before the mountainous shock
    The rank-ed gods dislock,
Scared to their skies; wide o'er rout-trampled night
Flew spurned the pebbled stars: those splendours then
   Had tempested on earth, star upon star
   Mounded in ruin, if a longer war
Had quaked Olympus and cold-fearing men.
    Then did the ample marge
    And circuit of thy targe
  Sullenly redden all the vaward fight,
    Above the blusterous clash
    Wheeled thy swung falchion's flash
  And hewed their forces into splintered flight.

Yet ere Olympus thou wast, and a god!
   Though we deny thy nod,
We cannot spoil thee of thy divinity.
   What know we elder than thee?
When thou didst, bursting from the great void's husk,
Leap like a lion on the throat o' the dusk;
   When the angels rose-chapleted
    Sang each to other,
   The vaulted blaze overhead
   Of their vast pinions spread,
    Hailing thee brother;
How chaos rolled back from the wonder,
And the First Morn knelt down to thy visage of thunder!
   Thou didst draw to thy side
   Thy young Auroral bride,
  And lift her veil of night and mystery;
   Tellus with baby hands
   Shook off her swaddling-bands,
  And from the unswath-ed vapours laughed to thee.

Thou twi-form deity, nurse at once and sire!
  Thou genitor that all things nourishest!
  The earth was suckled at thy shining breast,
And in her veins is quick thy milky fire.
Who scarfed her with the morning? and who set
Upon her brow the day-fall's carcanet?
    Who queened her front with the enrondured moon?
    Who dug night's jewels from their vaulty mine
     To dower her, past an eastern wizard's dreams,

When hovering on him through his haschish-swoon,
   All the rained gems of the old Tartarian line
Shiver in lustrous throbbings of tinged flame?
     Whereof a moiety in the Paolis' seams
     Statelily builded their Venetian name.
      Thou hast enwoof-ed her
       An empress of the air,
And all her births are propertied by thee:
      Her teeming centuries
       Drew being from thine eyes:
Thou fatt'st the marrow of all quality.

Who lit the furnace of the mammoth's heart?
  Who shagged him like Pilatus' ribb-ed flanks?
    Who raised the columned ranks
Of that old pre-diluvian forestry,
Which like a continent torn oppressed the sea,
  When the ancient heavens did in rains depart,
    While the high-danc-ed whirls
Of the tossed scud made hiss thy drench-ed curls?
     Thou rear'dst the enormous brood;
     Who hast with life imbued
    The lion maned in tawny majesty,
     The tiger velvet-barred,
     The stealthy-stepping pard,
    And the lithe panther's flexuous symmetry.

How came the entomb-ed tree a light-bearer,
    Though sunk in lightless lair?
    Friend of the forgers of earth,
   Mate of the earthquake and thunders volcanic,
   Clasped in the arms of the forces Titanic
    Which rock like a cradle the girth
     Of the ether-hung world;
   Swart son of the swarthy mine,
    When flame on the breath of his nostrils feeds
     How is his countenance half-divine,
     Like thee in thy sanguine weeds?
   Thou gavest him his light,
    Though sepultured in night
  Beneath the dead bones of a perished world;
   Over his prostrate form
   Though cold, and heat, and storm,
The mountainous wrack of a creation hurled.
    Who made the splendid rose

    Saturate with purple glows;
Cupped to the marge with beauty; a perfume-press
    Whence the wind vintages
Gushes of warm-ed fragrance richer far
 Than all the flavorous ooze of Cyprus' vats?
Lo, in yon gale which waves her green cymar,
    With dusky cheeks burnt red
    She sways her heavy head,
Drunk with the must of her own odorousness;
 While in a moted trouble the vexed gnats
Maze, and vibrate, and tease the noontide hush.
 Who girt dissolv-ed lightnings in the grape?
Summered the opal with an Irised flush?
 Is it not thou that dost the tulip drape,
   And huest the daffodilly,
   Yet who hast snowed the lily,
And her frail sister, whom the waters name,
 Dost vestal-vesture 'mid the blaze of June,
 Cold as the new-sprung girlhood of the moon
Ere Autumn's kiss sultry her cheek with flame?
   Thou sway'st thy sceptred beam
   O'er all delight and dream,
 Beauty is beautiful but in thy glance:
   And like a jocund maid
   In garland-flowers arrayed,
 Before thy ark Earth keeps her sacred dance.

And now, O shaken from thine antique throne,
  And sunken from thy coerule empery,
Now that the red glare of thy fall is blown
 In smoke and flame about the windy sky,
Where are the wailing voices that should meet
 From hill, stream, grove, and all of mortal shape
Who tread thy gifts, in vineyards as stray feet
 Pulp the globed weight of juiced Iberia's grape?
   Where is the threne o' the sea?
   And why not dirges thee
The wind, that sings to himself as he makes stride
 Lonely and terrible on the Andean height?
   Where is the Naiad 'mid her sworded sedge?
 The Nymph wan-glimmering by her wan fount's verge?
The Dryad at timid gaze by the wood-side?
   The Oread jutting light
 On one up-strain-ed sole from the rock-ledge?
   The Nereid tip-toe on the scud o' the surge,

With whistling tresses dank athwart her face,
And all her figure poised in lithe Circean grace?
  Why withers their lament?
  Their tresses tear-besprent,
 Have they sighed hence with trailing garment-gem?
  O sweet, O sad, O fair!
  I catch your flying hair,
Draw your eyes down to me, and dream on them!

A space, and they fleet from me. Must ye fade—
O old, essential candours, ye who made
  The earth a living and a radiant thing—
    And leave her corpse in our strained, cheated arms?
    Lo ever thus, when Song with chorded charms
Draws from dull death his lost Eurydice,
  Lo ever thus, even at consummating,
  Even in the swooning minute that claims her his,
  Even as he trembles to the impassioned kiss
  Of reincarnate Beauty, his control
  Clasps the cold body, and foregoes the soul!
    Whatso looks lovelily
Is but the rainbow on life's weeping rain.
Why have we longings of immortal pain,
And all we long for mortal? Woe is me,
And all our chants but chaplet some decay,
As mine this vanishing—nay, vanished Day.
The low sky-line dusks to a leaden hue,
  No rift disturbs the heavy shade and chill,
Save one, where the charred firmament lets through
  The scorching dazzle of Heaven; 'gainst which the hill,
    Out-flattened sombrely,
Stands black as life against eternity.
    Against eternity?
    A rifting light in me
Burns through the leaden broodings of the mind:
    O bless-ed Sun, thy state
    Uprisen or derogate
Dafts me no more with doubt; I seek and find.

  If with exultant tread
    Thou foot the Eastern sea,
    Or like a golden bee
 Sting the West to angry red,
  Thou dost image, thou dost follow
    That King-Maker of Creation,

Who, ere Hellas hailed Apollo,
   Gave thee, angel-god, thy station;
Thou art of Him a type memorial.
  Like Him thou hang'st in dreadful pomp of blood
    Upon thy Western rood;
  And His stained brow did veil like thine to night,
    Yet lift once more Its light,
And, risen, again departed from our ball,
But when It set on earth arose in Heaven.
Thus hath He unto death His beauty given:
And so of all which form inheriteth
   The fall doth pass the rise in worth;
For birth hath in itself the germ of death,
 But death hath in itself the germ of birth.
It is the falling acorn buds the tree,
The falling rain that bears the greenery,
  The fern-plants moulder when the ferns arise.
 For there is nothing lives but something dies,
And there is nothing dies but something lives.
   Till skies be fugitives,
Till Time, the hidden root of change, updries,
Are Birth and Death inseparable on earth;
For they are twain yet one, and Death is Birth.

AFTER-STRAIN

Now with wan ray that other sun of Song
  Sets in the bleakening waters of my soul:
One step, and lo! the Cross stands gaunt and long
  'Twixt me and yet bright skies, a presaged dole.

Even so, O Cross! thine is the victory.
  Thy roots are fast within our fairest fields;
Brightness may emanate in Heaven from thee,
  Here thy dread symbol only shadow yields.

Of reap-ed joys thou art the heavy sheaf
  Which must be lifted, though the reaper groan;
Yea, we may cry till Heaven's great ear be deaf,
  But we must bear thee, and must bear alone.

Vain were a Simon; of the Antipodes
  Our night not borrows the superfluous day.
Yet woe to him that from his burden flees!
  Crushed in the fall of what he cast away.

Therefore, O tender Lady, Queen Mary,
  Thou gentleness that dost enmoss and drape
The Cross's rigorous austerity,
  Wipe thou the blood from wounds that needs must gape.

'Lo, though suns rise and set, but crosses stay,
  I leave thee ever,' saith she, 'light of cheer.'
'Tis so: yon sky still thinks upon the Day,
  And showers aerial blossoms on his bier.

Yon cloud with wrinkled fire is edg-ed sharp;
  And once more welling through the air, ah me!
How the sweet viol plains him to the harp,
  Whose pang-ed sobbings throng tumultuously.

Oh, this Medusa-pleasure with her stings!
  This essence of all suffering, which is joy!
I am not thankless for the spell it brings,
  Though tears must be told down for the charmed toy.

No; while soul, sky, and music bleed together,
  Let me give thanks even for those griefs in me,
The restless windward stirrings of whose feather
  Prove them the brood of immortality.

My soul is quitted of death-neighbouring swoon,
  Who shall not slake her immitigable scars
Until she hear 'My sister!' from the moon,
  And take the kindred kisses of the stars.

A CAPTAIN OF SONG

(ON a portrait of Coventry Patmore by J. S. Sargent, R.A.)

    Look on him. This is he whose works ye know;
    Ye have adored, thanked, loved him,—no, not him!
    But that of him which proud portentous woe
    To its own grim
    Presentment was not potent to subdue,
    Nor all the reek of Erebus to dim.
    This, and not him, ye knew.
    Look on him now. Love, worship if ye can,
    The very man.
    Ye may not. He has trod the ways afar,
    The fatal ways of parting and farewell,
    Where all the paths of pain-ed greatness are;
    Where round and always round
    The abhorr-ed words resound,
    The words accursed of comfortable men,—
    'For ever'; and infinite glooms intolerable
    With spacious replication give again,
    And hollow jar,
    The words abhorred of comfortable men.
    You the stern pities of the gods debar
    To drink where he has drunk
    The moonless mere of sighs,
    And pace the places infamous to tell,
    Where God wipes not the tears from any eyes,
    Where-through the ways of dreadful greatness are
    He knows the perilous rout
    That all those ways about
    Sink into doom, and sinking, still are sunk.
    And if his sole and solemn term thereout
    He has attained, to love ye shall not dare
    One who has journeyed there;
    Ye shall mark well
    The mighty cruelties which arm and mar
    That countenance of control,
    With minatory warnings of a soul
    That hath to its own selfhood been most fell,
    And is not weak to spare:
    And lo, that hair
    Is blanch-ed with the travel-heats of hell.

    If any be

That shall with rites of reverent piety
Approach this strong
Sad soul of sovereign Song,
Nor fail and falter with the intimidate throng;
If such there be,
These, these are only they
Have trod the self-same way;
The never-twice-revolving portals heard
Behind them clang infernal, and that word
Abhorr-ed sighed of kind mortality,
As he—
Ah, even as he!

AGAINST URANIA

Lo I, Song's most true lover, plain me sore
That worse than other women she can deceive,
For she being goddess, I have given her more
Than mortal ladies from their loves receive;
And first of her embrace
She was not coy, and gracious were her ways,
That I forgot all virgins to adore;
Nor did I greatly grieve
To bear through arid days
The pretty foil of her divine delays;
And one by one to cast
Life, love, and health,
Content, and wealth,
Before her, thinking ever on her praise,
Until at last
Nought had I left she would be gracious for.
Now of her cozening I complain me sore,
Seeing her uses,
That still, more constantly she is pursued,
And straitlier wooed,
Her only-ador-ed favour more refuses,
And leaves me to implore
Remembered boon in bitterness of blood.

From mortal woman thou may'st know full well,
O poet, that dost deem the fair and tall
Urania of her ways not mutable,
When things shall thee befall
What thou art toil-ed in her sweet, wild spell.
Do they strow for thy feet
A little tender favour and deceit
Over the sudden mouth of hidden hell?—
As more intolerable
Her pit, as her first kiss is heavenlier-sweet.
Are they, the more thou sigh,
Still the more watchful-cruel to deny?—
Know this, that in her service thou shalt learn
How harder than the heart of woman is
The immortal cruelty
Of the high goddesses.
True is his witness who doth witness this,
Whose gaze too early fell—
Nor thence shall turn,
Nor in those fires shall cease to weep and burn—
Upon her ruinous eyes and ineludible.

AN ANTHEM OF EARTH

Proemion.
    Immeasurable Earth!
Through the loud vast and populacy of Heaven,
Tempested with gold schools of ponderous orbs,
That cleav'st with deep-revolting harmonies
Passage perpetual, and behind thee draw'st
A furrow sweet, a cometary wake
Of trailing music! What large effluence,
Not sole the cloudy sighing of thy seas,
Nor thy blue-coifing air, encases thee
From prying of the stars, and the broad shafts
Of thrusting sunlight tempers? For, dropped near
From my remov-ed tour in the serene
Of utmost contemplation, I scent lives.
This is the efflux of thy rocks and fields,
And wind-cuffed forestage, and the souls of men,
And aura of all treaders over thee;
A sentient exhalation, wherein close
The odorous lives of many-throated flowers,
And each thing's mettle effused; that so thou wear'st,
Even like a breather on a frosty morn,
Thy proper suspiration. For I know,
Albeit, with custom-dulled perceivingness,
Nestled against thy breast, my sense not take
The breathings of thy nostrils, there's no tree,
No grain of dust, nor no cold-seeming stone,
But wears a fume of its circumfluous self.
Thine own life and the lives of all that live,
The issue of thy loins,
Is this thy gaberdine,
Wherein thou walkest through thy large demesne
And sphery pleasances,—
Amazing the unstal-ed eyes of Heaven,
And us that still a precious seeing have
Behind this dim and mortal jelly.
    Ah!
If not in all too late and frozen a day
I come in rearward of the throats of song,
Unto the deaf sense of the ag-ed year
Singing with doom upon me; yet give heed!
One poet with sick pinion, that still feels
Breath through the Orient gateways closing fast,
Fast closing t'ward the undelighted night!

Anthem.

    In nescientness, in nescientness,
    Mother, we put these fleshly lendings on
    Thou yield'st to thy poor children; took thy gift
    Of life, which must, in all the after-days,
    Be craved again with tears,—
    With fresh and still-petitionary tears.
    Being once bound thine almsmen for that gift,
    We are bound to beggary, nor our own can call
    The journal dole of customary life,
    But after suit obsequious for't to thee.
    Indeed this flesh, O Mother,
    A beggar's gown, a client's badging,
    We find, which from thy hands we simply took,
    Nought dreaming of the after penury,
    In nescientness.

    In a little joy, in a little joy,
    We wear awhile thy sore insignia,
    Nor know thy heel o' the neck. O Mother! Mother!
    Then what use knew I of thy solemn robes,
    But as a child, to play with them? I bade thee
    Leave thy great husbandries, thy grave designs,
    Thy tedious state which irked my ignorant years,
    Thy winter-watches, suckling of the grain,
    Severe premeditation taciturn
    Upon the brooded Summer, thy chill cares,
    And all thy ministries majestical,
    To sport with me, thy darling. Thought I not
    Thou set'st thy seasons forth processional
    To pamper me with pageant,—thou thyself
    My fellow-gamester, appanage of mine arms?
    Then what wild Dionysia I, young Bacchanal,
    Danced in thy lap! Ah for thy gravity!
    Then, O Earth, thou rang'st beneath me,
    Rocked to Eastward, rocked to Westward,
    Even with the shifted
    Poise and footing of my thought!
    I brake through thy doors of sunset,
    Ran before the hooves of sunrise,
    Shook thy matron tresses down in fancies
    Wild and wilful
    As a poet's hand could twine them;
    Caught in my fantasy's crystal chalice
    The Bow, as its cataract of colours

Plashed to thee downward;
Then when thy circuit swung to nightward,
Night the abhorr-ed, night was a new dawning,
Celestial dawning
Over the ultimate marges of the soul;
Dusk grew turbulent with fire before me,
And like a windy arras waved with dreams.
Sleep I took not for my bedfellow,
Who could waken
To a revel, an inexhaustible
Wassail of orgiac imageries;
Then while I wore thy sore insignia
In a little joy, O Earth, in a little joy;
Loving thy beauty in all creatures born of thee,
Children, and the sweet-essenced body of woman;
Feeling not yet upon my neck thy foot,
But breathing warm of thee as infants breathe
New from their mother's morning bosom. So I,
Risen from thee, restless winnower of the heaven,
Most Hermes-like, did keep
My vital and resilient path, and felt
The play of wings about my fledg-ed heel—
Sure on the verges of precipitous dream,
Swift in its springing
From jut to jut of inaccessible fancies,
In a little joy.

In a little thought, in a little thought,
We stand and eye thee in a grave dismay,
With sad and doubtful questioning, when first
Thou speak'st to us as men: like sons who hear
Newly their mother's history, unthought
Before, and say—'She is not as we dreamed:
Ah me! we are beguiled!' What art thou, then,
That art not our conceiving? Art thou not
Too old for thy young children? Or perchance,
Keep'st thou a youth perpetual-burnishable
Beyond thy sons decrepit? It is long
Since Time was first a fledgling;
Yet thou may'st be but as a pendant bulla
Against his stripling bosom swung. Alack!
For that we seem indeed
To have slipped the world's great leaping-time, and come
Upon thy pinched and dozing days: these weeds,
These corporal leavings, thou not cast'st us new,

Fresh from thy craftship, like the lilies' coats,
But foist'st us off
With hasty tarnished piecings negligent,
Snippets and waste
From old ancestral wearings,
That have seen sorrier usage; remainder-flesh
After our father's surfeits; nay with chinks,
Some of us, that if speech may have free leave
Our souls go out at elbows. We are sad
With more than our sires' heaviness, and with
More than their weakness weak; we shall not be
Mighty with all their mightiness, nor shall not
Rejoice with all their joy. Ay, Mother! Mother!
What is this Man, thy darling kissed and cuffed,
Thou lustingly engender'st,
To sweat, and make his brag, and rot,
Crowned with all honour and all shamefulness?
From nightly towers
He dogs the secret footsteps of the heavens,
Sifts in his hands the stars, weighs them as gold-dust,
And yet is he successive unto nothing
But patrimony of a little mould,
And entail of four planks. Thou hast made his mouth
Avid of all dominion and all mightiness,
All sorrow, all delight, all topless grandeurs,
All beauty, and all starry majesties,
And dim transtellar things;—even that it may,
Filled in the ending with a puff of dust,
Confess—'It is enough.' The world left empty
What that poor mouthful crams. His heart is builded
For pride, for potency, infinity,
All heights, all deeps, and all immensities,
Arrased with purple like the house of kings,—
To stall the grey-rat, and the carrion-worm
Statelily lodge. Mother of mysteries!
Sayer of dark sayings in a thousand tongues,
Who bringest forth no saying yet so dark
As we ourselves, thy darkest! We the young,
In a little thought, in a little thought,
At last confront thee, and ourselves in thee,
And wake disgarmented of glory: as one
On a mount standing, and against him stands,
On the mount adverse, crowned with westering rays,
The golden sun, and they two brotherly
Gaze each on each;

He faring down
To the dull vale, his Godhead peels from him
Till he can scarcely spurn the pebble—
For nothingness of new-found mortality—
That mutinies against his gall-ed foot.
Littly he sets him to the daily way,
With all around the valleys growing grave,
And known things changed and strange; but he holds on,
Though all the land of light be widow-ed,
In a little thought.

In a little strength, in a little strength,
We affront thy unveiled face intolerable,
Which yet we do sustain.
Though I the Orient never more shall feel
Break like a clash of cymbals, and my heart
Clang through my shaken body like a gong;
Nor ever more with spurted feet shall tread
I' the winepresses of song; nought's truly lost
That moulds to sprout forth gain: now I have on me
The high Phoebean priesthood, and that craves
An unrash utterance; not with flaunted hem
May the Muse enter in behind the veil,
Nor, though we hold the sacred dances good,
Shall the holy Virgins maenadize: ruled lips
Befit a votaress Muse.
Thence with no mutable, nor no gelid love,
I keep, O Earth, thy worship,
Though life slow, and the sobering Genius change
To a lamp his gusty torch. What though no more
Athwart its roseal glow
Thy face look forth triumphal? Thou put'st on
Strange sanctities of pathos; like this knoll
Made derelict of day,
Couchant and shadow-ed
Under dim Vesper's overloosened hair:
This, where emboss-ed with the half-blown seed
The solemn purple thistle stands in grass
Grey as an exhalation, when the bank
Holds mist for water in the nights of Fall.
Not to the boy, although his eyes be pure
As the prime snowdrop is,
Ere the rash Phoebus break her cloister
Of sanctimonious snow;
Or Winter fasting sole on Himalay

Since those dove-nuncioed days
When Asia rose from bathing;
Not to such eyes,
Uneuphrasied with tears, the hierarchical
Vision lies unoccult, rank under rank
Through all create down-wheeling, from the Throne
Even to the bases of the pregnant ooze.
This is the enchantment, this the exaltation,
The all-compensating wonder,
Giving to common things wild kindred
With the gold-tesserate floors of Jove;
Linking such heights and such humilities
Hand in hand in ordinal dances,
That I do think my tread,
Stirring the blossoms in the meadow-grass,
Flickers the unwithering stars.
This to the shunless fardel of the world
Nerves my uncurb-ed back; that I endure,
The monstrous Temple's moveless caryatid,
With wide eyes calm upon the whole of things,
In a little strength.

In a little sight, in a little sight,
We learn from what in thee is credible
The incredible, with bloody clutch and feet
Clinging the painful juts of jagg-ed faith.
Science, old noser in its prideful straw,
That with anatomising scalpel tents
Its three-inch of thy skin, and brags—'All's bare,'
The eyeless worm, that boring works the soil,
Making it capable for the crops of God;
Against its own dull will
Ministers poppies to our troublous thought,
A Balaam come to prophecy,—parables,
Nor of its parable itself is ware,
Grossly unwotting; all things has expounded
Reflux and influx, counts the sepulchre
The seminary of being, and extinction
The Ceres of existence: it discovers
Life in putridity, vigour in decay;
Dissolution even, and disintegration,
Which in our dull thoughts symbolise disorder,
Finds in God's thoughts irrefragable order,
And admirable the manner of our corruption
As of our health. It grafts upon the cypress

The tree of Life—Death dies on his own dart
Promising to our ashes perpetuity,
And to our perishable elements
Their proper imperishability; extracting
Medicaments from out mortality
Against too mortal cogitation; till
Even of the caput mortuum we do thus
Make a memento vivere. To such uses
I put the blinding knowledge of the fool,
Who in no order seeth ordinance;
Nor thrust my arm in nature shoulder-high,
And cry—'There's nought beyond!' How should I so,
That cannot with these arms of mine engirdle
All which I am; that am a foreigner
In mine own region? Who the chart shall draw
Of the strange courts and vaulty labyrinths,
The spacious tenements and wide pleasances,
Innumerable corridors far-withdrawn,
Where I wander darkling, of myself?
Darkling I wander, nor I dare explore
The long arcane of those dim catacombs,
Where the rat memory does its burrows make,
Close-seal them as I may, and my stolen tread
Starts populace, a gens lucifuga;
That too strait seems my mind my mind to hold,
And I myself incontinent of me.
Then go I, my foul-venting ignorance
With scabby sapience plastered, aye forsooth!
Clap my wise foot-rule to the walls o' the world,
And vow—A goodly house, but something ancient,
And I can find no Master? Rather, nay,
By baffled seeing, something I divine
Which baffles, and a seeing set beyond;
And so with strenuous gazes sounding down,
Like to the day-long porer on a stream,
Whose last look is his deepest, I beside
This slow perpetual Time stand patiently,
In a little sight.

In a little dust, in a little dust,
Earth, thou reclaim'st us, who do all our lives
Find of thee but Egyptian villeinage.
Thou dost this body, this enhavocked realm,
Subject to ancient and ancestral shadows;
Descended passions sway it; it is distraught

With ghostly usurpation, dinned and fretted
With the still-tyrannous dead; a haunted tenement,
Peopled from barrows and outworn ossuaries.
Thou giv'st us life not half so willingly
As thou undost thy giving; thou that teem'st
The stealthy terror of the sinuous pard,
The lion maned with curl-ed puissance,
The serpent, and all fair strong beasts of ravin,
Thyself most fair and potent beast of ravin;
And thy great eaters thou, the greatest, eat'st.
Thou hast devoured mammoth and mastodon,
And many a floating bank of fangs,
The scaly scourges of thy primal brine,
And the tower-crested plesiosaure.
Thou fill'st thy mouth with nations, gorgest slow
On purple aeons of kings; man's hulking towers
Are carcase for thee, and to modern sun
Disglutt'st their splintered bones.
Rabble of Pharaohs and Arsacidae
Keep their cold house within thee; thou hast sucked down
How many Ninevehs and Hecatompyloi,
And perished cities whose great phantasmata
O'erbrow the silent citizens of Dis:-
Hast not thy fill?
Tarry awhile, lean Earth, for thou shalt drink,
Even till thy dull throat sicken,
The draught thou grow'st most fat on; hear'st thou not
The world's knives bickering in their sheaths? O patience!
Much offal of a foul world comes thy way,
And man's superfluous cloud shall soon be laid
In a little blood.

In a little peace, in a little peace,
Thou dost rebate thy rigid purposes
Of imposed being, and relenting, mend'st
Too much, with nought. The westering Phoebus' horse
Paws i' the lucent dust as when he shocked
The East with rising; O how may I trace
In this decline that morning when we did
Sport 'twixt the claws of newly-whelped existence,
Which had not yet learned rending? we did then
Divinely stand, not knowing yet against us
Sentence had passed of life, nor commutation
Petitioning into death. What's he that of
The Free State argues? Tellus! bid him stoop,

Even where the low hic jacet answers him;
Thus low, O Man! there's freedom's seignory,
Tellus' most reverend sole free commonweal,
And model deeply-policied: there none
Stands on precedence, nor ambitiously
Woos the impartial worm, whose favours kiss
With liberal largesse all; there each is free
To be e'en what he must, which here did strive
So much to be he could not; there all do
Their uses just, with no flown questioning.
To be took by the hand of equal earth
They doff her livery, slip to the worm,
Which lacqueys them, their suits of maintenance,
And that soiled workaday apparel cast,
Put on condition: Death's ungentle buffet
Alone makes ceremonial manumission;
So are the heavenly statutes set, and those
Uranian tables of the primal Law.
In a little peace, in a little peace,
Like fierce beasts that a common thirst makes brothers,
We draw together to one hid dark lake;
In a little peace, in a little peace,
We drain with all our burthens of dishonour
Into the cleansing sands o' the thirsty grave.
The fiery pomps, brave exhalations,
And all the glistering shows o' the seeming world,
Which the sight aches at, we unwinking see
Through the smoked glass of Death; Death, wherewith's fined
The muddy wine of life; that earth doth purge
Of her plethora of man; Death, that doth flush
The cumbered gutters of humanity;
Nothing, of nothing king, with front uncrowned,
Whose hand holds crownets; playmate swart o' the strong;
Tenebrous moon that flux and refluence draws
Of the high-tided man; skull-hous-ed asp
That stings the heel of kings; true Fount of Youth,
Where he that dips is deathless; being's drone-pipe;
Whose nostril turns to blight the shrivelled stars,
And thicks the lusty breathing of the sun;
Pontifical Death, that doth the crevasse bridge
To the steep and trifid God; one mortal birth
That broker is of immortality.
Under this dreadful brother uterine,
This kinsman feared, Tellus, behold me come,
Thy son stern-nursed; who mortal-motherlike,

To turn thy weanlings' mouth averse, embitter'st
Thine over-childed breast. Now, mortal-sonlike,
I thou hast suckled, Mother, I at last
Shall sustenant be to thee. Here I untrammel,
Here I pluck loose the body's cerementing,
And break the tomb of life; here I shake off
The bur o' the world, man's congregation shun,
And to the antique order of the dead
I take the tongueless vows: my cell is set
Here in thy bosom; my little trouble is ended
In a little peace.

MISCELLANEOUS POEMS

'EX ORE INFANTIUM'

Little Jesus, wast Thou shy
Once, and just so small as I?
And what did it feel like to be
Out of Heaven, and just like me?
Didst Thou sometimes think of THERE,
And ask where all the angels were?
I should think that I would cry
For my house all made of sky;
I would look about the air,
And wonder where my angels were;
And at waking 'twould distress me—
Not an angel there to dress me!
Hadst Thou ever any toys,
Like us little girls and boys?
And didst Thou play in Heaven with all
The angels that were not too tall,
With stars for marbles? Did the things
Play Can you see me? through their wings?
And did Thy Mother let Thee spoil
Thy robes, with playing on OUR soil?
How nice to have them always new
In Heaven, because 'twas quite clean blue!

Didst Thou kneel at night to pray,
And didst Thou join Thy hands, this way?
And did they tire sometimes, being young,
And make the prayer seem very long?
And dost Thou like it best, that we
Should join our hands to pray to Thee?
I used to think, before I knew,
The prayer not said unless we do.
And did Thy Mother at the night
Kiss Thee, and fold the clothes in right?
And didst Thou feel quite good in bed,
Kissed, and sweet, and thy prayers said?

Thou canst not have forgotten all
That it feels like to be small:
And Thou know'st I cannot pray
To Thee in my father's way—
When Thou wast so little, say,

Couldst Thou talk Thy Father's way?—
So, a little Child, come down
And hear a child's tongue like Thy own;
Take me by the hand and walk,
And listen to my baby-talk.
To Thy Father show my prayer
(He will look, Thou art so fair),
And say: 'O Father, I, Thy Son,
Bring the prayer of a little one.'

And He will smile, that children's tongue
Has not changed since Thou wast young!

A QUESTION

O bird with heart of wassail,
  That toss the Bacchic branch,
And slip your shaken music,
  An elfin avalanche;

Come tell me, O tell me,
  My poet of the blue!
What's YOUR thought of me, Sweet?—
  Here's MY thought of you.

A small thing, a wee thing,
  A brown fleck of nought;
With winging and singing
  That who could have thought?

A small thing, a wee thing,
  A brown amaze withal,
That fly a pitch more azure
  Because you're so small.

Bird, I'm a small thing—
  My angel descries;
With winging and singing
  That who could surmise?

Ah, small things, ah, wee things,
  Are the poets all,
Whose tour's the more azure
  Because they're so small.

The angels hang watching
  The tiny men-things:-
'The dear speck of flesh, see,
  With such daring wings!

'Come, tell us, O tell us,
  Thou strange mortality!
What's THY thought of us, Dear?—
  Here's OUR thought of thee.'

'Alack! you tall angels,
  I can't think so high!
I can't think what it feels like
  Not to be I.'

Come tell me, O tell me,
  My poet of the blue!
What's YOUR thought of me, Sweet?—
  Here's MY thought of you.

FIELD-FLOWER

A Phantasy.
    God took a fit of Paradise-wind,
      A slip of coerule weather,
    A thought as simple as Himself,
      And ravelled them together.
    Unto His eyes He held it there,
    To teach it gazing debonair
      With memory of what, perdie,
    A God's young innocences were.
    His fingers pushed it through the sod—
    It came up redolent of God,
    Garrulous of the eyes of God
      To all the breezes near it;
    Musical of the mouth of God
      To all had eyes to hear it;
    Mystical with the mirth of God,
      That glow-like did ensphere it.
        And—'Babble! babble! babble!' said;
          'I'll tell the whole world one day!'
      There was no blossom half so glad,
        Since sun of Christ's first Sunday.

A poet took a flaw of pain,
  A hap of skiey pleasure,
A thought had in his cradle lain,
  And mingled them in measure.
That chrism he laid upon his eyes,
And lips, and heart, for euphrasies,
  That he might see, feel, sing, perdie,
The simple things that are the wise.
Beside the flower he held his ways,
And leaned him to it gaze for gaze—
He took its meaning, gaze for gaze,
  As baby looks on baby;
Its meaning passed into his gaze,
  Native as meaning may be;
He rose with all his shining gaze
  As children's eyes at play be.
    And—'Babble! babble! babble!' said;
      'I'll tell the whole world one day!'
  There was no poet half so glad,
    Since man grew God that Sunday.

THE CLOUD'S SWAN-SONG

There is a parable in the pathless cloud,
There's prophecy in heaven,—they did not lie,
The Chaldee shepherds; seal-ed from the proud,
To cheer the weighted heart that mates the seeing eye.

A lonely man, oppressed with lonely ills,
And all the glory fallen from my song,
Here do I walk among the windy hills,
The wind and I keep both one monotoning tongue.

Like grey clouds one by one my songs upsoar
Over my soul's cold peaks; and one by one
They loose their little rain, and are no more;
And whether well or ill, to tell me there is none.

For 'tis an alien tongue, of alien things,
From all men's care, how miserably apart!
Even my friends say: 'Of what is this he sings?'
And barren is my song, and barren is my heart.

For who can work, unwitting his work's worth?
Better, meseems, to know the work for naught,
Turn my sick course back to the kindly earth,
And leave to ampler plumes the jetting tops of thought.

And visitations, that do often use,
Remote, unhappy, inauspicious sense
Of doom, and poets widowed of their muse,
And what dark 'gan, dark ended, in me did commence.

I thought of spirit wronged by mortal ills,
And my flesh rotting on my fate's dull stake;
And how self-scorn-ed they the bounty fills
Of others, and the bread, even of their dearest, take.

I thought of Keats, that died in perfect time,
In predecease of his just-sickening song;
Of him that set, wrapt in his radiant rhyme,
Sunlike in sea. Life longer had been life too long.

But I, exanimate of quick Poesy,—
O then, no more but even a soulless corse!
Nay, my Delight dies not; 'tis I should be

Her dead, a stringless harp on which she had no force.

Of my wild lot I thought; from place to place,
Apollo's song-bowed Scythian, I go on;
Making in all my home, with pliant ways,
But, provident of change, putting forth root in none.

Now, with starved brain, sick body, patience galled
With fardels even to wincing; from fair sky
Fell sudden little rain, scarce to be called
A shower, which of the instant was gone wholly by.

What cloud thus died I saw not; heaven was fair.
Methinks my angel plucked my locks: I bowed
My spirit, shamed; and looking in the air:-
'Even so,' I said, 'even so, my brother the good Cloud?'

It was a pilgrim of the fields of air,
Its home was allwheres the wind left it rest,
And in a little forth again did fare,
And in all places was a stranger and a guest.

It harked all breaths of heaven, and did obey
With sweet peace their uncomprehended wills;
It knew the eyes of stars which made no stay,
And with the thunder walked upon the lonely hills.

And from the subject earth it seemed to scorn,
It drew the sustenance whereby it grew
Perfect in bosom for the married Morn,
And of his life and light full as a maid kissed new.

Its also darkness of the face withdrawn,
And the long waiting for the little light,
So long in life so little. Like a fawn
It fled with tempest breathing hard at heel of flight;

And having known full East, did not disdain
To sit in shadow and oblivious cold,
Save what all loss doth of its loss retain,
And who hath held hath somewhat that he still must hold.

Right poet! who thy rightness to approve,
Having all liberty, didst keep all measure,
And with a firmament for ranging, move
But at the heavens' uncomprehended pleasure.

With amplitude unchecked, how sweetly thou
Didst wear the ancient custom of the skies,
And yoke of used prescription; and thence how
Find gay variety no license could devise!

As we the quested beauties better wit
Of the one grove our own than forests great,
Restraint, by the delighted search of it,
Turns to right scope. For lovely moving intricate

Is put to fair devising in the curb
Of ordered limit; and all-changeful Hermes
Is Terminus as well. Yet we perturb
Our souls for latitude, whose strength in bound and term is.

How far am I from heavenly liberty,
That play at policy with change and fate,
Who should my soul from foreign broils keep free,
In the fast-guarded frontiers of its single state!

Could I face firm the Is, and with To-be
Trust Heaven; to Heaven commit the deed, and do;
In power contained, calm in infirmity,
And fit myself to change with virtue ever new;

Thou hadst not shamed me, cousin of the sky,
Thou wandering kinsman, that didst sweetly live
Unnoted, and unnoted sweetly die,
Weeping more gracious song than any I can weave;

Which these gross-tissued words do sorely wrong.
Thou hast taught me on powerlessness a power;
To make song wait on life, not life on song;
To hold sweet not too sweet, and bread for bread though sour;

By law to wander, to be strictly free.
With tears ascended from the heart's sad sea,
Ah, such a silver song to Death could I
Sing, Pain would list, forgetting Pain to be,
And Death would tarry marvelling, and forget to die!

TO THE SINKING SUN

How graciously thou wear'st the yoke
  Of use that does not fail!
The grasses, like an anchored smoke,
  Ride in the bending gale;
This knoll is snowed with blosmy manna,
  And fire-dropt as a seraph's mail.

Here every eve thou stretchest out
  Untarnishable wing,
And marvellously bring'st about
  Newly an olden thing;
Nor ever through like-ordered heaven
  Moves largely thy grave progressing.

Here every eve thou goest down
  Behind the self-same hill,
Nor ever twice alike go'st down
  Behind the self-same hill;
Nor like-ways is one flame-sopped flower
  Possessed with glory past its will.

Not twice alike! I am not blind,
  My sight is live to see;
And yet I do complain of thy
  Weary variety.
O Sun! I ask thee less or more,
  Change not at all, or utterly!

O give me unprevisioned new,
  Or give to change reprieve!
For new in me is olden too,
  That I for sameness grieve.
O flowers! O grasses! be but once
  The grass and flower of yester-eve!

Wonder and sadness are the lot
  Of change: thou yield'st mine eyes
Grief of vicissitude, but not
  Its penetrant surprise.
Immutability mutable
  Burthens my spirit and the skies.

O altered joy, all joyed of yore,
  Plodding in unconned ways!
O grief grieved out, and yet once more
  A dull, new, staled amaze!
I dream, and all was dreamed before,
  Or dream I so? the dreamer says.

GRIEF'S HARMONICS

At evening, when the lank and rigid trees,
To the mere forms of their sweet day-selves drying,
On heaven's blank leaf seem pressed and flatten-ed;
Or rather, to my sombre thoughts replying,
Of plumes funereal the thin effigies;
That hour when all old dead things seem most dead,
And their death instant most and most undying,
That the flesh aches at them; there stirred in me
The babe of an unborn calamity,
Ere its due time to be deliver-ed.
Dead sorrow and sorrow unborn so blent their pain,
That which more present was were hardly said,
But both more NOW than any Now can be.
My soul like sackcloth did her body rend,
And thus with Heaven contend:-
'Let pass the chalice of this coming dread,
Or that fore-drained O bid me not re-drain!'
So have I asked, who know my asking vain,
Woe against woe in antiphon set over,
That grief's soul transmigrates, and lives again,
And in new pang old pang's incarnated.

MEMORAT MEMORIA

Come you living or dead to me, out of the silt of the Past,
With the sweet of the piteous first, and the shame of
    the shameful last?
Come with your dear and dreadful face through the passes of Sleep,
The terrible mask, and the face it masked—the face you did not keep?
You are neither two nor one—I would you were one or two,
For your awful self is embalmed in the fragrant self I knew:
And Above may ken, and Beneath may ken, what I mean by
    these words of whirl,
But by my sleep that sleepeth not,—O Shadow of a Girl!—
Nought here but I and my dreams shall know the secret of this thing:-
For ever the songs I sing are sad with the songs I never sing,
Sad are sung songs, but how more sad the songs we dare not sing!

Ah, the ill that we do in tenderness, and the hateful horror of love!
It has sent more souls to the unslaked Pit than it ever will draw above.
I damned you, girl, with my pity, who had better by far been thwart,
And drave you hard on the track to hell, because I was gentle of heart.
I shall have no comfort now in scent, no ease in dew, for this;
I shall be afraid of daffodils, and rose-buds are amiss;
You have made a thing of innocence as shameful as a sin,
I shall never feel a girl's soft arms without horror of the skin.
My child! what was it that I sowed, that I so ill should reap?
You have done this to me. And I, what I to you?—It lies with
Sleep.

JULY FUGITIVE

Can you tell me where has hid her
   Pretty Maid July?
I would swear one day ago
   She passed by,
I would swear that I do know
   The blue bliss of her eye:
'Tarry, maid, maid,' I bid her;
   But she hastened by.
Do you know where she has hid her,
   Maid July?

Yet in truth it needs must be
   The flight of her is old;
Yet in truth it needs must be,
   For her nest, the earth, is cold.
No more in the pool-ed Even
   Wade her rosy feet,
Dawn-flakes no more plash from them
   To poppies 'mid the wheat.
She has muddied the day's oozes
   With her petulant feet;
Scared the clouds that floated,
   As sea-birds they were,
Slow on the coerule
   Lulls of the air,
Lulled on the luminous
   Levels of air:
She has chidden in a pet
   All her stars from her;
Now they wander loose and sigh
   Through the turbid blue,
Now they wander, weep, and cry—
   Yea, and I too—
'Where are you, sweet July,
   Where are you?'

Who hath beheld her footprints,
   Or the pathway she goes?
Tell me, wind, tell me, wheat,
   Which of you knows?
Sleeps she swathed in the flushed Arctic
   Night of the rose?
Or lie her limbs like Alp-glow

On the lily's snows?
Gales, that are all-visitant,
   Find the runaway;
And for him who findeth her
   (I do charge you say)
I will throw largesse of broom
   Of this summer's mintage,
I will broach a honey-bag
   Of the bee's best vintage.
Breezes, wheat, flowers sweet,
   None of them knows!
How then shall we lure her back
   From the way she goes?
For it were a shameful thing,
   Saw we not this comer
Ere Autumn camp upon the fields
   Red with rout of Summer.

When the bird quits the cage,
   We set the cage outside,
With seed and with water,
   And the door wide,
Haply we may win it so
   Back to abide.
Hang her cage of earth out
   O'er Heaven's sunward wall,
Its four gates open, winds in watch
   By rein-ed cars at all;
Relume in hanging hedgerows
   The rain-quenched blossom,
And roses sob their tears out
   On the gale's warm heaving bosom;
Shake the lilies till their scent
   Over-drip their rims;
That our runaway may see
   We do know her whims:
Sleek the tumbled waters out
   For her travelled limbs;
Strew and smoothe blue night thereon,
   There will—O not doubt her!—
The lovely sleepy lady lie,
   With all her stars about her!

TO A SNOW-FLAKE

What heart could have thought you?—
Past our devisal
(O filigree petal!)
Fashioned so purely,
Fragilely, surely,
From what Paradisal
Imagineless metal,
Too costly for cost?
Who hammered you, wrought you,
From argentine vapour?—
'God was my shaper.
Passing surmisal,
He hammered, He wrought me,
From curled silver vapour,
To lust of His mind:-
Thou could'st not have thought me!
So purely, so palely,
Tinily, surely,
Mightily, frailly,
Insculped and embossed,
With His hammer of wind,
And His graver of frost.'

NOCTURN

I walk, I only,
Not I only wake;
Nothing is, this sweet night,
But doth couch and wake
For its love's sake;
Everything, this sweet night,
Couches with its mate.
For whom but for the stealthy-visitant sun
Is the naked moon
Tremulous and elate?
The heaven hath the earth
Its own and all apart;
The hush-ed pool holdeth
A star to its heart.
You may think the rose sleepeth,
But though she folded is,
The wind doubts her sleeping;
Not all the rose sleeps,
But smiles in her sweet heart
For crafty bliss.
The wind lieth with the rose,
And when he stirs, she stirs in her repose:
The wind hath the rose,
And the rose her kiss.
Ah, mouth of me!
Is it then that this
Seemeth much to thee?—
I wander only.
The rose hath her kiss.

A MAY BURDEN

Through meadow-ways as I did tread,
The corn grew in great lustihead,
And hey! the beeches burgeon-ed.
   By Godd-es fay, by Godd-es fay!
It is the month, the jolly month,
It is the jolly month of May.

God ripe the wines and corn, I say
And wenches for the marriage-day,
And boys to teach love's comely play.
   By Godd-es fay, by Godd-es fay!
It is the month, the jolly month,
It is the jolly month of May.

As I went down by lane and lea,
The daisies reddened so, pardie!
'Blushets!' I said, 'I well do see,
   By Godd-es fay, by Godd-es fay!
The thing ye think of in this month,
Heigho! this jolly month of May.'

As down I went by rye and oats,
The blossoms smelt of kisses; throats
Of birds turned kisses into notes;
   By Godd-es fay, by Godd-es fay!
The kiss it is a growing flower,
I trow, this jolly month of May!

God send a mouth to every kiss,
Seeing the blossom of this bliss
By gathering doth grow, certes!
   By Godd-es fay, by Godd-es fay!
Thy brow-garland pushed all aslant
Tells—but I tell not, wanton May!

   NOTE. The first two stanzas are from a French original—I have forgotten what.

A DEAD ASTRONOMER

(FATHER Perry, S.J.)

    Starry amorist, starward gone,
    Thou art—what thou didst gaze upon!
    Passed through thy golden garden's bars,
    Thou seest the Gardener of the Stars.

    She, about whose moon-ed brows
    Seven stars make seven glows,
    Seven lights for seven woes;
    She, like thine own Galaxy,
    All lustres in one purity:-
    What said'st thou, Astronomer,
    When thou did'st discover HER?
    When thy hand its tube let fall,
    Thou found'st the fairest Star of all!

'CHOSE VUE'

A metrical caprice.

> Up she rose, fair daughter—well she was graced
> As a cloud her going, stept from her chair,
> As a summer-soft cloud, in her going paced,
> Down dropped her riband-band, and all her waving hair
> Shook like loosened music cadent to her waist;—
> Lapsing like music, wavery as water,
>   Slid to her waist.

'WHERETO ART THOU COME?'

'Friend, whereto art thou come?' Thus Verity;
Of each that to the world's sad Olivet
Comes with no multitude, but alone by night,
Lit with the one torch of his lifted soul,
Seeking her that he may lay hands on her;
Thus: and waits answer from the mouth of deed.
Truth is a maid, whom men woo diversely;
This, as a spouse; that, as a light-o'-love,
To know, and having known, to make his brag.
But woe to him that takes the immortal kiss,
And not estates her in his housing life,
Mother of all his seed! So he betrays,
Not Truth, the unbetrayable, but himself:
And with his kiss's rated traitor-craft,
The Haceldama of a plot of days
He buys, to consummate his Judasry
Therein with Judas' guerdon of despair.

HEAVEN AND HELL

'Tis said there were no thought of hell,
   Save hell were taught; that there should be
A Heaven for all's self-credible.
   Not so the thing appears to me.
'Tis Heaven that lies beyond our sights,
   And hell too possible that proves;
For all can feel the God that smites,
   But ah, how few the God that loves!

TO A CHILD

Whenas my life shall time with funeral tread
The heavy death-drum of the beaten hours,
Following, sole mourner, mine own manhood dead,
Poor forgot corse, where not a maid strows flowers;
When I you love am no more I you love,
But go with unsubservient feet, behold
Your dear face through changed eyes, all grim change prove;—
A new man, mock-ed with misname of old;
When shamed Love keep his ruined lodging, elf!
When, ceremented in mouldering memory,
Myself is hears-ed underneath myself,
And I am but the monument of me:-
   O to that tomb be tender then, which bears
   Only the name of him it sepulchres!

HERMES

Soothsay. Behold, with rod twy-serpented,
Hermes the prophet, twining in one power
The woman with the man. Upon his head
The cloudy cap, wherewith he hath in dower
The cloud's own virtue—change and counterchange,
To show in light, and to withdraw in pall,
As mortal eyes best bear. His lineage strange
From Zeus, Truth's sire, and maiden May—the all-
Illusive Nature. His fledged feet declare
That 'tis the nether self transdeified,
And the thrice-furnaced passions, which do bear
The poet Olympusward. In him allied
  Both parents clasp; and from the womb of Nature
  Stern Truth takes flesh in shows of lovely feature.

HOUSE OF BONDAGE

I

    When I perceive Love's heavenly reaping still
    Regard perforce the clouds' vicissitude,
    That the fixed spirit loves not when it will,
    But craves its seasons of the flawful blood;
    When I perceive that the high poet doth
    Oft voiceless stray beneath the uninfluent stars,
    That even Urania of her kiss is loath,
    And Song's brave wings fret on their sensual bars;
    When I perceived the fullest-sail-ed sprite
    Lag at most need upon the leth-ed seas,
    The provident captainship oft voided quite,
    And lam-ed lie deep-draughted argosies;
        I scorn myself, that put for such strange toys
        The wit of man to purposes of boys.

II

    The spirit's ark sealed with a little clay,
    Was old ere Memphis grew a memory; [3]
    The hand pontifical to break away
    That seal what shall surrender? Not the sea
    Which did englut great Egypt and his war,
    Nor all the desert-drown-ed sepulchres.
    Love's feet are stained with clay and travel-sore,
    And dusty are Song's lucent wing and hairs.
    O Love, that must do courtesy to decay,
    Eat hasty bread standing with loins up-girt,
    How shall this stead thy feet for their sore way?
    Ah, Song, what brief embraces balm thy hurt!
        Had Jacob's toil full guerdon, casting his
        Twice-seven heaped years to burn in Rachel's kiss?

---

[3] The Ark of the Egyptian temple was sealed with clay, which the Pontiff-king broke when he entered the inner shrine to offer worship.

THE HEART

TWO Sonnets.

(To my Critic, who had objected to the phrase—'The heart's burning floors.')

I

The heart you hold too small and local thing,
Such spacious terms of edifice to bear.
And yet, since Poesy first shook out her wing,
The mighty Love has been impalaced there;
That has she given him as his wide demesne,
And for his sceptre ample empery;
Against its door to knock has Beauty been
Content; it has its purple canopy
A dais for the sovereign lady spread
Of many a lover, who the heaven would think
Too low an awning for her sacred head.
The world, from star to sea, cast down its brink—
   Yet shall that chasm, till He Who these did build
   An awful Curtius make Him, yawn unfilled.

II

O nothing, in this corporal earth of man,
That to the imminent heaven of his high soul
Responds with colour and with shadow, can
Lack correlated greatness. If the scroll
Where thoughts lie fast in spell of hieroglyph
Be mighty through its mighty habitants;
If God be in His Name; grave potence if
The sounds unbind of hieratic chants;
All's vast that vastness means. Nay, I affirm
Nature is whole in her least things exprest,
Nor know we with what scope God builds the worm.
Our towns are copied fragments from our breast;
   And all man's Babylons strive but to impart
   The grandeurs of his Babylonian heart.

A SUNSET

FROM Hugo's 'Feuilles d'Automne'.
>I love the evenings, passionless and fair, I love the evens,
>Whether old manor-fronts their ray with golden fulgence leavens,
>In numerous leafage bosomed close;
>Whether the mist in reefs of fire extend its reaches sheer,
>Or a hundred sunbeams splinter in an azure atmosphere
>On cloudy archipelagos.
>
>Oh gaze ye on the firmament! a hundred clouds in motion,
>Up-piled in the immense sublime beneath the winds' commotion,
>Their unimagined shapes accord:
>Under their waves at intervals flames a pale levin through,
>As if some giant of the air amid the vapours drew
>A sudden elemental sword.
>
>The sun at bay with splendid thrusts still keeps the sullen fold;
>And momently at distance sets, as a cupola of gold,
>The thatched roof of a cot a-glance;
>Or on the blurred horizons joins his battle with the haze;
>Or pools the glooming fields about with inter-isolate blaze
>Great moveless meres of radiance.
>
>Then mark you how there hangs athwart the firmament's swept track
>Yonder a mighty crocodile with vast irradiant back,
>A triple row of pointed teeth?
>Under its burnished belly slips a ray of eventide,
>The flickerings of a hundred glowing clouds its tenebrous side
>With scales of golden mail ensheathe.
>
>Then mounts a palace, then the air vibrates—the vision flees.
>Confounded to its base, the fearful cloudy edifice
>Ruins immense in mounded wrack:
>Afar the fragments strew the sky, and each envermeiled cone
>Hangeth, peak downward, overhead, like mountains overthrown
>When the earthquake heaves its hugy back.
>
>These vapours with their leaden, golden, iron, bronz-ed glows,
>Where the hurricane, the waterspout, thunder, and hell repose,
>Muttering hoarse dreams of destined harms,
>'Tis God who hangs their multitude amid the skiey deep,
>As a warrior that suspendeth from the roof-tree of his keep
>His dreadful and resounding arms!

All vanishes! The sun, from topmost heaven precipitated,
Like to a globe of iron which is tossed back fiery red
Into the furnace stirred to fume,
Shocking the cloudy surges, plashed from its impetuous ire,
Even to the zenith spattereth in a flecking scud of fire
The vaporous and inflam-ed spume.

O contemplate the heavens! whenas the vein-drawn day dies pale,
In every season, every place, gaze through their every veil,
With love that has not speech for need;
Beneath their solemn beauty is a mystery infinite:
If winter hue them like a pall; or if the summer night
Fantasy them with starry brede.

HEARD ON THE MOUNTAIN

FROM Hugo's 'Feuilles d'Automne'.

    Have you sometimes, calm, silent, let your tread aspirant rise
    Up to the mountain's summit, in the presence of the skies?
    Was't on the borders of the South? or on the Bretagne coast?
    And at the basis of the mount had you the Ocean tossed?
    And there, leaned o'er the wave and o'er the immeasurableness,
    Calm, silent, have you harkened what it says? Lo, what it says!
    One day at least, whereon my thought, enlicens-ed to muse,
    Had drooped its wing above the beach-ed margent of the ooze,
    And, plunging from the mountain height into the immensity,
    Beheld upon one side the land, on the other side the sea.
    I harkened, comprehended,—never, as from those abysses,
    No, never issued from a mouth, nor moved an ear, such voice as this is!

    A sound it was, at outset, vast, immeasurable, confused,
    Vaguer than is the wind among the tufted trees effused,
    Full of magnificent accords, suave murmurs, sweet as is
    The evensong, and mighty as the shock of panoplies
    When the hoarse melee in its arms the closing squadrons grips,
    And pants, in furious breathings, from the clarions' brazen lips.
    Unutterable the harmony, unsearchable its deep,
    Whose fluid undulations round the world a girdle keep,
    And through the vasty heavens, which by its surges are washed young,
    Its infinite volutions roll, enlarging as they throng,
    Even to the profound arcane, whose ultimate chasms sombre
    Its shattered flood englut with time, with space and form and number.
    Like to another atmosphere with thin o'erflowing robe,
    The hymn eternal covers all the inundated globe:
    And the world, swathed about with this investuring symphony,
    Even as it trepidates in the air, so trepidates in the harmony.

    And pensive, I attended the ethereal lutany,
    Lost within this containing voice as if within the sea.

    Soon I distinguished, yet as tone which veils confuse and smother,
    Amid this voice two voices, one commingled with the other,
    Which did from off the land and seas even to the heavens aspire;
    Chanting the universal chant in simultaneous quire.
    And I distinguished them amid that deep and rumorous sound,
    As who beholds two currents thwart amid the fluctuous profound.

    The one was of the waters; a be-radiant hymnal speech!
    That was the voice o' the surges, as they parleyed each with each.

The other, which arose from our abode terranean,
Was sorrowful; and that, alack! the murmur was of man;
And in this mighty quire, whose chantings day and night resound,
Every wave had its utterance, and every man his sound.

Now, the magnificent Ocean, as I said, unbannering
A voice of joy, a voice of peace, did never stint to sing,
Most like in Sion's temples to a psaltery psaltering,
And to creation's beauty reared the great lauds of his song.
Upon the gale, upon the squall, his clamour borne along
Unpausingly arose to God in more triumphal swell;
And every one among his waves, that God alone can quell,
When the other of its song made end, into the singing pressed.
Like that majestic lion whereof Daniel was the guest,
At intervals the Ocean his tremendous murmur awed;
And I, t'ward where the sunset fires fell shaggily and broad,
Under his golden mane, methought, that I saw pass the hand of God.

Meanwhile, and side by side with that august fan-faronnade,
The other voice, like the sudden scream of a destrier affrayed,
Like an infernal door that grates ajar its rusty throat,
Like to a bow of iron that gnarls upon an iron rote,
Grinded; and tears, and shriekings, the anathema, the lewd taunt,
Refusal of viaticum, refusal of the font,
And clamour, and malediction, and dread blasphemy, among
That hurtling crowd of rumour from the diverse human tongue,
Went by as who beholdeth, when the valleys thick t'ward night,
The long drifts of the birds of dusk pass, blackening flight on flight.
What was this sound whose thousand echoes vibrated unsleeping?
Alas! the sound was earth's and man's, for earth and man were weeping.

Brothers! of these two voices, strange most unimaginably,
Unceasingly regenerated, dying unceasingly,
Harken-ed of the Eternal throughout His Eternity,
The one voice uttereth: NATURE! and the other voice: HUMANITY!

Then I alit in reverie; for my ministering sprite
Alack! had never yet deployed a pinion of an ampler flight,
Nor ever had my shadow endured so large a day to burn:
And long I rested dreaming, contemplating turn by turn
Now that abyss obscure which lurked beneath the water's roll,
And now that other untemptable abyss which opened in my soul.
And I made question of me, to what issues are we here,
Whither should tend the thwarting threads of all this ravelled gear;
What doth the soul; to be or live if better worth it is;

And why the Lord, Who, only, reads within that book of His,
In fatal hymeneals hath eternally entwined
The vintage-chant of nature with the dirging cry of humankind?

(The metre of the second of these two translations is an experiment. The splendid fourteen-syllable metre of Chapman I have treated after the manner of Drydenian rhyming heroics; with the occasional triplet, and even the occasional Alexandrine, represented by a line of eight accents—a treatment which can well extend, I believe, the majestic resources of the metre.)

ULTIMA

LOVE'S ALMSMAN PLAINETH HIS FARE

O you, love's mendicancy who never tried,
  How little of your almsman me you know!
Your little languid hand in mine you slide,
  Like to a child says—'Kiss me and let me go!'
And night for this is fretted with my tears,
  While I:-'How soon this heavenly neck doth tire
Bending to me from its transtellar spheres!'
  Ah, heart all kneaded out of honey and fire!
Who bound thee to a body nothing worth,
  And shamed thee much with an unlovely soul,
That the most strainedest charity of earth
  Distasteth soon to render back the whole
Of thine inflam-ed sweets and gentilesse!
  Whereat, like an unpastured Titan, thou
Gnaw'st on thyself for famine's bitterness,
  And leap'st against thy chain. Sweet Lady, how
Little a linking of the hand to you!
  Though I should touch yours careless for a year,
Not one blue vein would lie divinelier blue
  Upon your fragile temple, to unsphere
The seraphim for kisses! Not one curve
  Of your sad mouth would droop more sad and sweet.
But little food love's beggars needs must serve,
  That eye your plenteous graces from the street.
A hand-clasp I must feed on for a night,
  A noon, although the untasted feast you lay,
To mock me, of your beauty. That you might
  Be lover for one space, and make essay
What 'tis to pass unsuppered to your couch,
  Keep fast from love all day; and so be taught
The famine which these craving lines avouch!
  Ah! miser of good things that cost thee naught,
How know'st thou poor men's hunger?—Misery!
When I go doleless and unfed by thee!

A HOLOCAUST

'No man ever attained supreme knowledge, unless his heart had been torn up by the roots.'

When I presage the time shall come—yea, now
  Perchance is come, when you shall fail from me,
Because the mighty spirit, to whom you vow
  Faith of kin genius unrebukably,
Scourges my sloth, and from your side dismissed
  Henceforth this sad and most, most lonely soul
Must, marching fatally through pain and mist,
  The God-bid levy of its powers enrol;
When I presage that none shall hear the voice
  From the great Mount that clangs my ordained advance,
That sullen envy bade the churlish choice
  Yourself shall say, and turn your altered glance;
O God! Thou knowest if this heart of flesh
  Quivers like broken entrails, when the wheel
Rolleth some dog in middle street, or fresh
  Fruit when ye tear it bleeding from the peel;
If my soul cries the uncomprehended cry
  When the red agony oozed on Olivet!
Yet not for this, a caitiff, falter I,
  Beloved whom I must lose, nor thence regret
The doubly-vouched and twin allegiance owed
  To you in Heaven, and Heaven in you, Lady.
How could you hope, loose dealer with my God,
  That I should keep for you my fealty?
For still 'tis thus:-because I am so true,
My Fair, to Heaven, I am so true to you!

BENEATH A PHOTOGRAPH

Phoebus, who taught me art divine,
Here tried his hand where I did mine;
And his white fingers in this face
Set my Fair's sigh-suggesting grace.
O sweetness past profaning guess,
Grievous with its own exquisiteness!
Vesper-like face, its shadows bright
With meanings of sequestered light;
Drooped with shamefast sanctities
She purely fears eyes cannot miss,
Yet would blush to know she IS.
Ah, who can view with passionless glance
This tear-compelling countenance!
He has cozened it to tell
Almost its own miracle.
Yet I, all-viewing though he be,
Methinks saw further here than he;
And, Master gay! I swear I drew
Something the better of the two!

AFTER HER GOING

The after-even! Ah, did I walk,
  Indeed, in her or even?
For nothing of me or around
  But absent She did leaven,
Felt in my body as its soul,
  And in my soul its heaven.

'Ah me! my very flesh turns soul,
  Essenced,' I sighed, 'with bliss!'
And the blackbird held his lutany,
  All fragrant-through with bliss;
And all things stilled were as a maid
  Sweet with a single kiss.

For grief of perfect fairness, eve
  Could nothing do but smile;
The time was far too perfect fair,
  Being but for a while;
And ah, in me, too happy grief
  Blinded herself with smile!

The sunset at its radiant heart
  Had somewhat unconfest:
The bird was loath of speech, its song
  Half-refluent on its breast,
And made melodious toyings with
  A note or two at best.

And she was gone, my sole, my Fair,
  Ah, sole my Fair, was gone!
Methinks, throughout the world 'twere right
  I had been sad alone;
And yet, such sweet in all things' heart,
  And such sweet in my own!

MY LADY THE TYRANNESS

Me since your fair ambition bows
Feodary to those gracious brows,
Is nothing mine will not confess
Your sovran sweet rapaciousness?
Though use to the white yoke inures,
Half-petulant is
Your loving rebel for somewhat his,
Not yours, my love, not yours!

Behold my skies, which make with me
One passionate tranquillity!
Wrap thyself in them as a robe,
She shares them not; their azures probe,
No countering wings thy flight endures.
Nay, they do stole
Me like an aura of her soul.
I yield them, love, for yours!

But mine these hills and fields, which put
Not on the sanctity of her foot.
Far off, my dear, far off the sweet
Grave pianissimo of your feet!
My earth, perchance, your sway abjures?—
Your absence broods
O'er all, a subtler presence. Woods,
Fields, hills, all yours, all yours!

Nay then, I said, I have my thought,
Which never woman's reaching raught;
Being strong beyond a woman's might,
And high beyond a woman's height,
Shaped to my shape in all contours.—
I looked, and knew
No thought but you were garden to.
All yours, my love, all yours!

Meseemeth still, I have my life;
All-clement Her its resolute strife
Evades; contained, relinquishing
Her mitigating eyes; a thing
Which the whole girth of God secures.
Ah, fool, pause! pause!
I had no life, until it was

All yours, my love, all yours!

Yet, stern possession! I have my death,
Sole yielding up of my sole breath;
Which all within myself I die,
All in myself must cry the cry
Which the deaf body's wall immures.—
Thought fashioneth
My death without her.—Ah, even death
All yours, my love, all yours!

Death, then, he hers. I have my heaven,
For which no arm of hers has striven;
Which solitary I must choose,
And solitary win or lose.—
Ah, but not heaven my own endures!
I must perforce
Taste you, my stream, in God your source,—
So steep my heaven in yours.

At last I said—I have my God,
Who doth desire me, though a clod,
And from His liberal Heaven shall He
Bar in mine arms His privacy.
Himself for mine Himself assures.—
None shall deny
God to be mine, but He and I
All yours, my love, all yours!

I have no fear at all lest I
Without her draw felicity.
God for His Heaven will not forego
Her whom I found such heaven below,
And she will train Him to her lures.
Nought, lady, I love
In you but more is loved above;
What made me, makes Him yours.

'I, thy sought own, am I forgot?'
Ha, thou?—thou liest, I seek thee not.
Why what, thou painted parrot, Fame,
What have I taught thee but her name?
Hear, thou slave Fame, while Time endures,
I give her thee;
Page her triumphal name!—Lady,
Take her, the thrall is yours.

UNTO THIS LAST

A boy's young fancy taketh love
Most simply, with the rind thereof;
A boy's young fancy tasteth more
The rind, than the deific core.
Ah, Sweet! to cast away the slips
Of unessential rind, and lips
Fix on the immortal core, is well;
But heard'st thou ever any tell
Of such a fool would take for food
Aspect and scent, however good,
Of sweetest core Love's orchards grow?
Should such a phantast please him so,
Love where Love's reverent self denies
Love to feed, but with his eyes,
All the savour, all the touch,
Another's—was there ever such?
Such were fool, if fool there be;
Such fool was I, and was for thee!
But if the touch and savour too
Of this fruit—say, Sweet, of you—
You unto another give
For sacrosanct prerogative,
Yet even scent and aspect were
Some elected Second's share;
And one, gone mad, should rest content
With memory of show and scent;
Would not thyself vow, if there sigh
Such a fool—say, Sweet, as I—
Treble frenzy it must be
Still to love, and to love thee?

Yet had I torn (man knoweth not,
Nor scarce the unweeping angels wot
Of such dread task the lightest part)
Her fingers from about my heart.
Heart, did we not think that she
Had surceased her tyranny?
Heart, we bounded, and were free!
O sacrilegious freedom!—Till
She came, and taught my apostate will
The winnowed sweet mirth cannot guess
And tear-fined peace of hopefulness;
Looked, spake, simply touched, and went.

Now old pain is fresh content,
Proved content is unproved pain.
Pangs fore-tempted, which in vain
I, faithless, have denied, now bud
To untempted fragrance and the mood
Of contrite heavenliness; all days
Joy affrights me in my ways;
Extremities of old delight
Afflict me with new exquisite
Virgin piercings of surprise,—
Stung by those wild brown bees, her eyes!

ULTIMUM

Now in these last spent drops, slow, slower shed,
Love dies, Love dies, Love dies—ah, Love is dead!
Sad Love in life, sore Love in agony,
Pale Love in death; while all his offspring songs,
Like children, versed not in death's chilly wrongs,
About him flit, frighted to see him lie
So still, who did not know that Love could die.
One lifts his wing, where dulls the vermeil all
Like clotting blood, and shrinks to find it cold,
And when she sees its lapse and nerveless fall
Clasps her fans, while her sobs ooze through the webb-ed gold.
Thereat all weep together, and their tears
Make lights like shivered moonlight on long waters.
Have peace, O piteous daughters!
He shall not wake more through the mortal years,
Nor comfort come to my soul widow-ed,
Nor breath to your wild wings; for Love is dead!

I slew, that moan for him: he lifted me
Above myself, and that I might not be
Less than myself, need was that he should die;
Since Love that first did wing, now clogged me from the sky.
Yet lofty Love being dead thus passeth base—
There is a soul of nobleness which stays,
The spectre of the rose: be comforted,
Songs, for the dust that dims his sacred head!
The days draw on too dark for Song or Love;
O peace, my songs, nor stir ye any wing!
For lo, the thunder hushing all the grove,
And did Love live, not even Love could sing.

And, Lady, thus I dare to say,
Not all with you is passed away!
For your love taught me this:-'tis Love's true praise
To be, not staff, but writ of worthy days;
And that high worth in love unfortunate
Should still remain it learned in love elate.
Beyond your star, still, still the stars are bright;
Beyond your highness, still I follow height;
Sole I go forth, yet still to my sad view,
Beyond your trueness, Lady, Truth stands true.
This wisdom sings my song with last firm breath,
Caught from the twisted lore of Love and Death,

The strange inwoven harmony that wakes
From Pallas' straying locks twined with her aegis-snakes.
'On him the unpetitioned heavens descend,
Who heaven on earth proposes not for end;
The perilous and celestial excess
Taking with peace, lacking with thankfulness.
Bliss in extreme befits thee not, until
Thou'rt not extreme in bliss; be equal still:
Sweets to be granted think thy self unmeet
Till thou have learned to hold sweet not too sweet.'
This thing not far is he from wise in art
Who teacheth; nor who doth, from wise in heart.

ENVOY

Go, songs, for ended is our brief, sweet play;
  Go, children of swift joy and tardy sorrow:
And some are sung, and that was yesterday,
  And some unsung, and that may be to-morrow.

Go forth; and if it be o'er stony way,
  Old joy can lend what newer grief must borrow:
And it was sweet, and that was yesterday,
  And sweet is sweet, though purchas-ed with sorrow.

Go, songs, and come not back from your far way:
  And if men ask you why ye smile and sorrow,
Tell them ye grieve, for your hearts know To-day,
  Tell them ye smile, for your eyes know To-morrow.

Echo Library
www.echo-library.com

Echo Library uses advanced digital print-on-demand technology to build and preserve an exciting world class collection of rare and out-of-print books, making them readily available for everyone to enjoy.

Situated just yards from Teddington Lock on the River Thames, Echo Library was founded in 2005 by Tom Cherrington, a specialist dealer in rare and antiquarian books with a passion for literature.

Please visit our website for a complete catalogue of our books, which includes foreign language titles.

The Right to Read

Echo Library actively supports the Royal National Institute for the Blind's Right to Read initiative by publishing a comprehensive range of Large Print (16 point Tiresias font as recommended by the RNIB) and Clear Print (13 point Tiresias font) titles for those who find standard print difficult to read.

Customer Service

If there is a serious error in the text or layout please send details to feedback@echo-library.com and we will supply a corrected copy. If there is a printing fault or the book is damaged please refer to your supplier.

CPSIA information can be obtained at www.ICGtesting.com
Printed in the USA
BVOW012014141111

276092BV00004B/25/A